Where there's a Bill there's a Way

To John
enjoy ~ Bill

Where there's a Bill there's a Way

Bill Furlong

TRICORN
BOOKS

www.tricornbooks.co.uk

Where there's a Bill there's a Way
Bill Furlong

Published by Tricorn Books
Design © 131 Design Ltd
www.131design.org
Text © Bill Furlong

A CIP catalogue record for this book is available from the
British Library.

ISBN 978-0-9571074-8-9

Published 2012 by
Tricorn Books
a trading name of
131 Design Ltd
131 High Street
Old Portsmouth
PO1 2HW
www.tricornbooks.co.uk

Printed & bound in UK by Berforts Group Ltd

To Lorna and all the kind people
who have been kind to me.

Contents

Foreword

Written in his own words, Bill Furlong's story is of growing up in Portsmouth with autism in the 70s and 80s. Whilst Bill was clinically diagnosed with the condition when he was a child, he did not realise or understand what it was that made him different until he was 32 years old when he experienced a Eureka moment:

> *... I began to write, it eventually turned to my past experiences. As I wrote the words, their symmetry began to take on a pattern and a new realisation began to form. You're autistic, a voice screamed; liberating me from what? I began to write more and more, faster and faster about my life and experiences, aching, a kind of euphoria.*

This book is the culmination of that writing and is published in Bill's own words, providing a unique insight into an autistic mind. His writing has not been edited, regularised or smoothed out to trip off the tongue; it has deliberately been kept as Bill wrote it, and demands the reader give their full attention so as not to trip and stumble, the way Bill has done, often. Whilst dead-pan, the emotions it evokes are raw and blunt, sometimes making you feel like you've been hit by a double-decker bus, as you read what you fear and what you know is true.

Bill grapples to understand not only what is happening to him, but also the consequences and effect his behaviour has on those around him, and how best to deal with it. Mostly, Bill gets it wrong.

Not only does Bill wrestle to understand himself but he faces a constant struggle to understand the behaviour of others, as well as the norms in society that most of us take for granted and which moderate our behaviour. It is a totally honest, or rather frank account of events because Bill doesn't lie, or know what a lie is, just as he doesn't know how to moderate his behaviour to be acceptable.

Starting when he was at junior school, Bill goes on to chart his experiences at mainstream middle school, senior school and college where he faced constant torment, highlighting what can happen and often does happen to those with differences in mainstream education. As a young man in the work place, his experience was only marginally better.

Bill sometimes struggles to explain the confusion in his head, but states with utmost clarity what it is like to be autistic and constantly living in a mental fog. This he terms as being mentally deaf, dumb and blind. He spends large amounts of time, dissecting his behaviour and trying to understand what is wrong and why, and it is only with hindsight and his own personal development that he is able to reflect on and understand the absurdity of his behaviour, as well as the ignorance of those around him.

Sometimes it is heartbreakingly hilarious in its candour, sometimes it is hard reading in its sadness and sometimes, it is intense in its overwhelmingness, but in all that, it is a real page turner that takes you on an enlightening journey of his life through his eyes.

Chapter 1

Just Bill

I was six; it was 1971. I am autistic.

Six was the age I was supposed to have started to behave oddly. Between six and eleven, I was supposed to have been more adventurous than my brother; I went off on my own to Cosham by bus. Are autistic people more adventurous than others? Are they more prepared to explore the world in order to make up for being cut off from it?

When I was eleven I was wandering the streets round our house in the early afternoons and evenings. I was walking up one road one day, the road leading up to the hill overlooking Portsmouth as I was planning to walk along the edge of the hill, when a boy with long, dark hair stood in front of me and would not let me pass. He wanted me to do the 'Tetley Tea folk dance'; this was a dance performed by cartoon characters in a television advert. If I tried to get past him he slapped my face.

The shock was too great for me to retaliate; it was too sudden. I could not punch him directly, not just because I was too timid but also because I could not really work out whether it was acceptable socially. It was as if my social and physical consciousnesses were not working in conjunction together. My social consciousness might not have been properly developed at this stage to be able to deal with a confrontation like this.

Many years later, between the ages of eighteen and thirty, I would have dealt with this by saying, 'I was just walking up this road when you stood in my way. Will you please move aside?' As for what he tried to make me do, I would have said, 'I don't want to do what you want. I'll do what I want to do. It's a strange thing to stop someone and want them to do a silly dance.' When he slapped me, I would have hit back or I would have threatened to go to the police.

He claimed, in this particular incident and on other occasions, that I had sworn at him. I believed, from what my parents and others had told me, in turning the other cheek. I confused turning the other cheek verbally, i.e. ignoring insults, with turning the other cheek in a literal and physical sense, and ignoring physical abuse. I wanted to stand up for myself but did not know how to.

At the bottom of an alley where this bully once cornered me, I tried expressing myself to him. I tried to talk about rights and prerogatives, but it just came out as nonsense.

'He's a divvy, isn't he?' the bully said incredulously to a boy who had been passing and intervened. What had come out of my mouth must have seemed bizarre to him. 'Divvy' was the term he used to describe me.

I managed to get away from him that time but there were other times he would beat me up.

My parents, especially my father, urged me to fight back. 'One day you'll discover what a nasty vicious place this world is, so you thump that kid,' he had urged. Talking about how nasty and vicious my father claimed the world seemed to be, sounded corny and trite at the time.

'If word gets round that you allowed this kid to thump you, other kids will see you and know you're easy meat,' my father had said over the dinner table. I knew what he said made sense but did not want to accept it.

'They can't eat me,' I replied, addressing his use of the term, 'easy meat,' which also struck me as trite. A friend of the family, the mother in a family called the Greens, told me to hit back.

'When you see that boy, you hit him,' she said.

When I saw him, I ran away. I felt not just fear, but also pain, as though he represented something that was too unpleasant for me to face.

My brother asked me if the boy was bigger than me; he was not.

Eventually the boy went away: his family may have moved out of the area or he was sent to a borstal. I did not see him again.

I did not have any friends in the area. The only people I spent any time with were my family and the two brothers who were friends of my brother, Nick and Simon Green. I would try going around with them but they were older than me and soon got fed up with me. I could not decide whether I even wanted any friends my own age.

I was attending Court Lane Middle School and had not actually done much work there, if any at all. I would start copying something out at my desk but then my focus would trail off. My teachers frequently shouted at me. They would be shouting something about my work, and pointing furiously at my textbooks but I did not really understand what they were shouting about, or even saying to me.

I had one teacher called Mr Powell who would frequently yell at me, once yelling, 'You should be smacked through every inch of your life!'

My father blamed Mr Powell for not shouting at me enough when I was about ten or eleven.

'If I ever see that Mr Powell again, I'm going to be rather rude to that man,' was how strongly my father felt about what he saw as a crucial stage in my life, and the influence Mr Powell should have had on it. He thought it was important that a teacher try to get through to me.

Another teacher by the same name, a lady called Miss Powell, figured prominently at this time. There was one occasion when she ordered us to get our textbooks out but I could not find mine. Miss Powell asked me why my textbook was not in front of me. I looked at her, then I looked in my desk, and under the table, and all around it. Finally, I looked at her, 'I'm awfully sorry,' I said, in a posh manner, 'but I can't seem to find it.' Miss Powell was not angry, but the class collapsed in hysterics.

I cannot recall being intentionally or unintentionally funny, nor can I totally recall the laughter from the class, I only got an impression. I talked in a posh, precise manner because it was what I thought showed correct behaviour, stability and maturity. Miss Powell must have sensed that I was not trying to be clever or cheeky, she was just slightly baffled. It was my way of being precocious and my way of acting slightly superior.

My concentration was bad, not just when applied to work, but in other ways too. One time, a teacher sent me into the corridor to open some windows and to this day, looking back, I do not know what windows she wanted me to open – the windows of the classroom, or the windows of the corridor. I wandered round the corridor looking into the classroom. Eventually, I came back to the classroom to get yelled at by the teacher.

This particular teacher was a hot-tempered, volatile woman whom I was nervous of. I was nervous of an incident like the windows in the corridor because she had a fiery temperament.

'I'm sorry I'm dreamy,' I blurted out.

'Yes, you are dreamy,' she snapped in mid rage.

The French teacher said I mumbled between my lips. I do not know whether this was something I did when I was by myself, or when I was reciting French that he was referring to. According to my parents, I would whisper to myself at home. Another habit I had, according to my parents, was going up to people and looking them in the eyes while standing a few inches from their face.

My family got concerned and impatient when I could not concentrate. I would not help properly with the washing up. They complained about me not remembering where the cutlery belonged, or going off into my own world and not helping at all. My family frequently told me about my 'little acts', when I would do a lot of strange movements and mannerisms while dancing around.

'You're going to have to buck your ideas up,' my father had told me one day at the dinner table. 'In six years time, you'll be on the job market,' or words to that effect.

Chapter 2

Assessment time

*I*nevitably I was sent to see someone; inevitably it was a child psychologist – a child psychiatrist was probably reserved for more serious cases.

I first had some tests performed on me involving me putting marbles in a cup when I heard a sound in some earphones. I was told afterwards that I was perfectly intelligent. That statement is frequently made about a child or adult displaying strange behaviour, as though whether they are intelligent or not has any relevance to this.

I was sent to a place called…….. There I met a tall, benign man, aged forty-seven who wore glasses. His name was Maurice Bridgeland and he would be my best friend for twenty-three years plus. We later started meeting at his clinic in a road called Battenberg Avenue, located in an area just after North End in Portsmouth.

I went to see Maurice at the clinic until 1992 when he retired. I must have enjoyed talking to him and seeing him for the same reason I enjoy talking to him now on the phone, and enjoy talking to many psychologists and psychiatrists; he seemed on my intellectual level.

My mother would take me to see him. We would meet in a room that was adorned with pictures on the walls painted by children, there would be toys on the floor and near the walls.

In fact, it was just how a child psychologist's room would be imagined.

My conversations with Maurice were erratic, according to him. I was far less relaxed than other children my own age. We would be talking when I would suddenly ask him, 'Have you ever read *Frankenstein*?' That probably baffled Maurice; he would later use this as an example to show how oddly I had behaved.

I recall Maurice, in his usual casual way, asking me why I asked that question. He told me I had frequently got up and walked around the room, walking on one spot. It was a variation of my 'little acts' that my mother mentioned to me. The 'little acts' as a physical activity were, and are, possibly physical expressions of physical energy, the energy not expressed in positive acceptable ways but being expressed according to however the person concerned, or I in this case, wanted to express it.

The autistic mind does not perceive and acknowledge socially acceptable behaviour. It does not consciously or sub-consciously know the correct way to express energy. Conventional expressions of energy can take the form of working on an interest or project, or walking around socialising; the autistic mind cannot apply conventional mental processes. Instead, in my case, and the case of some other autistic children, the energy was expressed through my 'little acts', and sadly some other autistic children's head-banging, screaming and fits. In the course of 23 years and as many as 5,00 visits to Maurice, I managed to control my strange movements when I was seeing him.

I told him about my being bullied by the local boy. If I had been too confused to fight back it was tragic, he said. Tragic in my case and in the case of many other children and adults who have a mental handicap, severe enough to make them vulnerable. If they are vulnerable, it is because they are confused, and their confusion makes them too timid to be assertive.

It was about mid-infancy that I had started to have problems of being 'aware of what was around me,' as my father would say. I could see and hear perfectly but had become mentally deaf, dumb and blind (MDDB). The longer I continued being MDDB, the harder it would be for me to start to think and be more aware, not just mentally but also physically.

My developmental process had been somehow distracted. I did not mingle and associate with children my own age, and thus did not come to share their understanding of the world. The ages six to eleven are supposed to be important because they are such impressionable ages. My mother told me I was very well behaved up to the age of six, I did not run around on my own and I did not 'play up'.

Being very well behaved up to that age is supposed to be a classic autistic sign. Autistic children are supposed to demand a structured system, or set of rituals. I had no set of rituals but I did insist, however, on a lot of 'sameness', which became habitual.

There was a time I went through when I was very pliable to other people's suggestions and very subservient. Other children would tell me to do something, like stand on one leg, or stand in a particular spot and I would do it. I remember some of it happening in the playground and later occurring outside school.

It had started as what I perceived to be normal childhood behaviour, like the sort of games children play, but because an autistic person cannot understand what they are 'permitted' to do and can not carry out what is socially acceptable, they are susceptible to misunderstanding the expectations of others.

Word got round about my strange attitude. In Burrill Avenue, just beside Southdown Road where we lived, I overheard a group of children I was standing near. They were saying I would do anything I was told. One of the children told me to go and stand in a particular spot. I was more reluctant than usual to do this and I was slower in doing it, possibly because I had heard them talking about me, and I was embarrassed. But I had actually processed social information!

I began to do what others told me to do less often; it may have been part of wanting to be 'accepted' that I had done it in the first place. Subconsciously, I had wanted friends from an early age. I had wanted to have them so, like my brother with Mike and Nick Green, I could find things out about the world around me with them, and have fun with them.

It could be embarrassing for me when I went around with a group of boys because of the way they claimed I talked, and of what I said. I talked in a very posh voice and flowery way, and expressed myself in what I thought was an intellectual manner. I once said something with a group of kids that got amused comments from them. I made a joke.

My time at Manor Court Middle School was stressful. It was stressful because of the way I perceived how I was treated, as much as the actual way I was treated. Girls would tease me; I was a solitary figure and girls tend to notice people like that. The boys and girls were probably teasing each other all the time but the teasing I got from the girls was more upsetting because it was sexual. Many of the girls and many of the boys seemed sexually more aware than I was then.

They once asked me, 'Are you a virgin?' I did not hear this properly and thought they asked, 'Are you a first year?' – as in a first year student.

'No,' I replied. 'I'm a second year.' The group of girls concerned broke down into hysterics.

Another incident I can remember from Manor Court was one in assembly. I had thought of something I found very funny and burst out laughing, the only problem was the school was singing a hymn at the time. I realised something was wrong when Mr Pearson, the headmaster, looked at me. I had done it partly because I thought I could get away with it; it wasn't something like talking to another pupil in class or assembly that I thought I could get away with, it was laughing out loud to myself. But the way I laughed filled the hall, according to one pupil I later met.

Afterwards, Mr Pearson came forward and pointed me out, ordering me to come to his staffroom later. I went and stood outside his staffroom and waited for what seemed an eternity; I think I was supposed to have gone back to my classroom first. When Mr Pearson came and found me standing outside his staffroom, he just said something about how I should have been attending some lesson.

I got off the assembly incident through the flimsy excuse that it was my way of enjoying the hymn. Pearson probably had other things to do and he sent me away. He muttered something like, 'And next time, use your brains!' with reference to how I had missed some sort of class time while standing outside his office.

I was later angry with him for inferring that I had not 'used my brains', as at the time I considered myself quite intelligent, so was he referring to some contradiction?

Just after he had ordered me to his office, the other kids had clustered round me as we broke from assembly. They seemed concerned as to where I thought the staffroom was and enquired if I understood what I had to do. Their concern seemed like the concern for someone they felt was different from them, different and needing help.

When I got back to the classroom, the teacher herself was angry with me. 'You naughty boy!' she shouted.

I later remembered thinking that Pearson had already reprimanded me, so why was she so angry? Maybe I did not understand the cause and effect of my behaviour, just as I did not understand its implications. Was she partly angry because I had missed class time? This also made me angry.

As I began to turn thirteen, it was discussed whether I should go to a special school or a normal school. I understood my own feelings about my condition, my feeling odd and alienated, but I did not understand the feelings of others. If I had gone to a special school, it most probably would have been Cliffdale. Cliffdale was the main, if only, special school for the Portsmouth area. It was often mentioned as a kind of insult amongst the kids I had been with. It was the place where all the educationally subnormal, the mentally handicapped children were sent. It was mentioned as a sort of embarrassed joke amongst kids, or a source of ignorant hostility. 'You went to Cliffdale,' was a standard insult. I had definitely heard of Cliffdale but I did not know where it was. Most of the other kids at Manor Court knew where Cliffdale was.

Maurice knew me; he had known me and spoken to me for a long time. He said I was a child of above average intelligence who, if I went to Cliffdale, would be amongst children whose intelligence was definitely below mine.

As my father once stated, 'We were going to send you to a special school.' He then enquired, 'What do you think of that?'

I did not think much about it at all. I did not see any irony or contradiction in an intelligent child being considered stupid. I was considered stupid because my behaviour seemed strange to others. A lot of children coming up to thirteen would have been perturbed at being sent to a special school. Ironically, if I had been aware of the type of school they almost sent me to, I would not have been eligible to be sent. I was also unaware of the implications of being unaware. Maurice once told me that if I had been sent to a special school, I would have been treated as abnormal for the rest of my life – I would be treated as abnormal anyway for the next ten years, if not intermittently for the rest of my entire life.

A special school would definitely not extend my educational opportunities, whereas a conventional school would. The children who went to special schools tended to have levels of intelligence that were fixed from birth. These levels of intelligence could be a lot more difficult to improve than someone with an active level of autism but average, or below average, intelligence. However, by the time I had finished school at sixteen, I had improved sufficiently to undertake GCSEs, or 'O' levels as they were then called. Maurice Bridgeland had always refused to support my going to a special school like Cliffdale and he was instrumental in having me sent to a 'normal' school. Social and emotional factors can also improve a person's intelligence and responses, whether they are autistic or not.

At home, up until I was twelve or thirteen, I was chided for being too introspective. 'You're too introspective and introverted,' my father had told me. When I stated how I was feeling, which was frequently, it was usually negative; I was only seeing myself from my own perspective.

Because I had no friends, my mother had tried to introduce me to someone; he was younger than me and was an alternative to Nick and Simon, my brother's friends. My lack of friends was obviously due in part to my introspection.

'You've got to ask yourself, am I cold? No. Am I hungry? No.' My father posed these questions to me and went on to answer them as me, 'Then what the hell am I worrying about? I've got my health!'

My introspection, the very thing that made me friendless, could have been helped by me making friends. My father, anxious about what he considered my lack of awareness, had complained violently that, 'He doesn't realise what an absolute struggle life is!'

I had a vague idea of what my father meant. I had had a glimpse of the absolute social reality my father talked about, but my awareness of it had not been permanent. It had not developed into a total, 'World View' that other people's awareness normally developed into.

My brother had some similar problems to me at school, namely not working hard enough and just sitting at his desk. His reports from his teachers were bad enough, but not as bad as mine. His period of non-compliance seemed only temporary. My reports were so bad that my father had taken me into the living room and said, 'We need to do some Maths and English during the school holidays and evenings to catch up.'

We both settled down to study Maths and English. My English could be improved in the way I wrote the actual words, using tracing paper over rows of joined Os and Cs and Ts. My maths was very different. I would sit next to my father and he would try to explain arithmetic and other elements, such as factors but he would end up thundering at me, 'And five eights make forty and six eights make forty eight!' I would be scared because he seemed to get so impatient and aggressive. He was getting angry so quickly and I did not know why. I was bad at Maths then, but the basic principles such as factors I now understand, despite them being shouted in my ear. It was a piece of information I could not immediately understand, and when it was applied forcefully, it scared me. If it had been taught in school a different way, involving for example soldiers, or battles or with a reference point, I might have understood. My work at school began to improve, in part because there was more of it.

My father used to get impatient with me hanging around the house, particularly in my room, not doing anything. My activity was playing with soldiers. I would buy boxes of plastic soldiers and arrange them for fighting. Maurice would have said this was an expression of frustration, coupled with an inner desire for something; I myself would have said it was something I just enjoyed doing.

It was at twelve years of age that I started using a knife and fork. At meal times, I would eat with my fingers as we sat round the table; my family kept complaining about this. I found chips and sausages easiest to eat with my fingers. I suppose I used my fingers because either I could not be bothered to use a knife and fork, or could not understand how to use them. I had not naturally observed and processed the fact that my family used knives and forks, thus obliging me to follow suit. It was a classic case of what Maurice later called, 'Not knowing how other people work,' by which he meant not knowing what other people would be thinking in a certain situation about certain things.

I played with soldiers until I was thirteen; I did not realise playing with soldiers may be construed as childish by some people because I had no conception of their values. Let us say, I had been going around Cosham with a group of boys and exploring all its streets, and we had been going over Cosham Hill and everywhere. Let us say, myself, or one of these boys, aged between ten or eleven, had said or done something childish and the other boys had mocked and derided us, or more importantly, said it was childish. I might have understood if I had been with a group of boys my own age. I might have actually learnt in time what behaviour was considered childish and what was not. By the age of ten do children learn what is childish and what is not? The answer is that some learn more quickly than others what is considered childish and what is considered mature. They moderate their behaviour according to their peer groups and so become young adults more quickly.

There was an incident on Cosham Hill when I heard some older boys denigrate some younger boys because of their behaviour and there were other incidents when I heard older boys mocking infants for throwing sharp points, such as school compasses, in the air. As children grow older, their awareness of any relative immaturity grows. As I was only an onlooker, not a participant, I was unable to share any of their thinking.

I had been judged to be mentally advanced enough academically to attend a conventional school, rather than a special one. I had no real learning disabilities when it came to academia, yet, if someone had asked me my age, up to when I was sixteen, I would not have known. I had learnt through television and other children about jets, Kung Fu, skydiving and a lot of the other things children are supposed to be interested in, but they couldn't tell me about my age.

I never imagined myself in situations such as being a jet pilot. I never considered taking up Kung Fu either, then or when I was older. I never seriously considered being anything, because I could not imagine myself in the world. I had considered the world around me, subconsciously, and had rejected it. The shock of self-realisation had been too great for me to endure. The shock of absolute responsibility had been too much of a shock.

Chapter 3

A Normal School

*M*y parents had hoped I would not be bullied at Springfield Comprehensive, the school I was destined for, and like most conventional comprehensive schools it was large, with many pupils. It was so large and had so many people, it was impossible for me to make friends there. It would have been difficult for anyone, but for me, it was much more so.

'If you're bullied, tell someone,' my mother said.

'If you're bullied, you thump them,' my father said in contrast.

My father dropped me off by car, just inside the school gate. 'Got everything?' he had asked. I nodded and stepped out of the car into my next three years of education.

The first day was hectic, all the teachers having to find classes for all the boys and girls. To me it was all confusion and noise, a blur of movement and voices.

I had few social reference points. There was no-one I knew going to the school, apart from my brother, as I had made no friends beforehand. Later, on the first day, a boy had come up to me and told me to bend over. I did so and he then kicked me in the backside to try and make me fall over. I did not realise what he was going to do, as I did not even realise he had come up to me. After I had recovered myself, there in a part of the school that was in front of many other kids, I asked him why he had done what he did. I felt a sudden hard blow; a few minutes later I realised he had punched me in the mouth. I did not know what to do; I began to cry. I was shocked. Some girls who seemed to be concerned, crowded round me. Reporting him would be a lot easier, I decided at the time, than fighting him. The girls urged me to tell someone as I began to walk away.

The boy caught up with me. 'Sorry mate. Don't tell anyone will you?' Was it acceptable to forgive someone for something like hitting you in the face if they say sorry? At the time I did not exactly forgive him, I just gave in to what he wanted.

My social functioning and my social maturity affected my social responses. I was still pliable, and whilst I would hesitate to do everything others told me to, I would go along with some of it. I was no longer so ready to do everything I was told, like go and stand in a particular spot, but I was still very influenced by what other people wanted, especially teachers.

Of course, I should have punched the other kid from the outset, to establish myself; it was what my father had kept urging me to do. But hitting the boy would have meant the trouble of having a fight, as well as encountering trouble with the teachers. Also, though I knew what my father meant about establishing a reputation, establishing a reputation would have meant establishing a reputation in the other children's minds, based on what influenced their thinking. But I had not grasped what influenced their thinking at the time. I knew it in my head but I did not have a complete understanding of it as a social factor.

My brother had once asked me directly whether I was afraid of authority, too afraid to get into trouble through justifiable action. I had once told a teacher I had felt like hitting someone who had been annoying me.

'Oh, no. You mustn't do that,' she insisted. 'People have got into trouble and been suspended for fighting.' I knew teachers had authority and that because their authority was justified, it was always to be obeyed. I saw that as a simple rule. I did not realise that some rules can be circumnavigated in some situations. A teacher might privately condone a boy punching a bully in self-defence or under extreme provocation, but he or she may not say it openly. However, this is the only way I could have understood as I did not understand unspoken social factors.

Sometimes I was more afraid of the teachers than the children whom I thought might attack me. I would often ask my brother what particular teachers were like, meaning were they very aggressive and loud? Did they shout much in class?

In one early morning incident, a month into being at the school, I had an argument with another boy. There had been talk of a fight between us and the other kids had heard about it. They had got both of us together in one of the toilets while they gathered round, excited at the prospect of violence. I got upset and almost started crying. A teacher, who happened to be passing, entered the toilets and demanded to know what was going on. Seeing my nervous state, he thought I was being bullied – he was probably right, so he marched us all off to the Deputy Head's office. I stood there frightened and distraught; the Deputy Head's shouting terrified me more than any bullying.

'What's he ever done to you lot?' the Deputy Head demanded of them. He was attacking them in the interest of my welfare but at the same time shouting. Shouting like this was a form of communication I was not used to and did not like. Autistic people can find social communication painful anyway, whether it is talking or having to listen. In this case it was being delivered in an aggressive and powerful way.

We were finally dismissed. I found the experience of hearing the boys punished more frightening than what I had experienced earlier in the toilets, surrounded by boys, chanting, 'Fight. Fight.'

The fight incident was in the same month that I lost my timetable for my lessons. My form tutor had automatically snapped when she heard this.

'You're an idiot,' her voice cracked. 'Only an idiot would lose all his timetables. You're a work problem,' she thundered, getting out another sheet from the desk for me to fill out.

I had started to feel bad after she snapped the first time, and then I began to cry. Not many people noticed but I had experienced something even more painful than seeing and hearing aggression, being subject to it. Seeing angry faces and hearing loud voices directed at me was worse than observing them from the outside. Also, the speed at which my form tutor snapped and acted upset me. She had snapped so quickly, I had not had time to adjust to it mentally and emotionally. My crying at being shouted at was unaffected by how I thought other children might perceive me, because I had no understanding of how they may have perceived it. That children can perceive crying as childish in response to being shouted at had not yet entered my head.

My reputation for being odd might have been from boys and girls seeing me in the Cosham area with my peculiar mannerisms and they might have passed the word round, which could have then gone on to Springfield. My reputation for being odd at school might also have been because of the way other pupils saw me in my first few weeks at Springfield and noticed the way I walked and acted, and the way I immediately struck people. Those that saw me called me 'Doolally' at school. Some used the term rather casually, others used it less pleasantly. If I had spent time with the boys, they might have begun to use the term as an affectionate nickname, if they did not already.

'All right, Doolally,' they would say as I entered a toilet. They would be grouped at one end, all in miscellaneous school uniforms, with different combinations of ties and shirts.

The term 'Doolally' originally referred to the Deolali transit camp in India where British soldiers passed through before going home in the Second World War. They often had a long wait before ships returned them to England and the severe heat and extreme boredom could create psychological problems for some soldiers. In these cases, it was said that they had 'gone Doolally', meaning they had gone a bit mad. Since then, the term 'Doolally' had entered British slang, meaning insane or mad.

I had anticipated that in my first weeks of going to Springfield I would be feeling odd and different from the others, and because I had anticipated it, it did not hurt all that much.

Once, in the toilets, a boy had grabbed hold of my shoulder while I was washing my hands.

'Hiya, Doolally,' he had glowered. This was one of the few times it had been meant truly hurtfully.

At school I tried to avoid certain people who I thought had somehow attacked me or who intended to attack me. Once, when trying to avoid such a group, I had ducked down, running with my back and head bent downwards, through another group of kids, around a wall. Unfortunately, the group of boys I was trying to avoid, who had been giving me funny responses and calling me Doolally, saw me. Very soon, to my regret, the seven or eight boys came rushing past me. They were led by a tall, shorthaired boy and were all imitating my absurd run, while smirking at me. My absurd run was not only an attempt to avoid certain people seeing me, but it also showed my inability to imitate the correct social posture of others. If I had anticipated and thought how my posture would look, I could have decided not to do it. My attempt to avoid trouble had led to looking odd, which had thus led to more trouble.

There were other incidents that created social embarrassments in my first week of Springfield. On my first day, in addition to being punched, I had asked another pupil where the toilets were. It was a perfectly normal question to me, but if the lad was new as well, he was also precocious and mischievous. He muttered a few things and then said, 'Go in the bushes,' and walked off with a smirk. I stood, and seriously considered going in the bushes that dotted the school. I wandered round for a bit then began to unzip my fly in one clump of bushes. At the very last moment a girl shouted out, 'No!' to me. She might have been a friend of my brother's.

'You weren't actually going to do it were you?' my brother had groaned. The girl had said something similar, and redirected me to the proper toilets.

The bushes were part of school property, and would only half hide a person from the prying eyes of other children. At the time I had known bushes and undergrowth could be used as a toilet if they were in particular places, such as beside a road or in the countryside. When I had heard the boy say, 'Go in the bushes,' it was a combination of literal interpretation based on what I knew already, and understanding what was appropriate for a physical situation. Also, I had not fully realised the boy was joking or kidding me when he said it.

The way people are flippant, whether in the rather cruel

way that the boy was, or flippant when they become adults, was beyond my processing. I observed it, or a variation of it, in the playground when children played; I had not however, processed or understood it when directed at myself.

I had taken part in flippant exchanges a few times, or rather tried to take part in them a few times. My trying to imitate others' flippancy had only caused laughter. For example, I had observed children pretending to be monsters like Dracula and Frankenstein when I was at Manor Court School but had been too embarrassed to do it myself. This behaviour was not odd to the children who performed it because it was mutually agreed and shared. However, any child who behaved that way on their own might have been considered more than a little odd. The only games I had played had been games involving soldiers and armies, which were games that to me were more real and more disciplined.

I had played a game of 'Cavalry and Indians' with a very good lad called Mark Winter. I was later told that he had always liked me and was one of the few friends I had. I had got to know him locally before discovering that he went to the same school as me. Games like Cavalry and Indians gave me a feeling of power and control. Once, when a group of kids had not played the game the way I wanted, I got really upset.

That was all in the past though, amongst ten-to-twelve-year-olds; now I was at comprehensive school with people in their early to mid teens. One of the things I was curious about was why these kids were not playing the sort of games I had observed at middle school. It was a sort of behaviour I had observed long enough to feel like imitating, but I realised now, it was too late. These pupils, in their process of social maturity, had moved on and left me behind them.

In the first week of Springfield, I along with all the other pupils had been given homework to do. I had wanted to do it to get it over with. It was assigned to me in the morning and I had been roaming round the school, looking for somewhere to do it. There were no empty classrooms for me to go to, as there would be for students in the sixth form or college, so instead, I got my exercise book and pen out and started writing up my homework, leaning against the side of a school building. It was the side of the school's swimming pool building and it had a roof protruding from the top. The roof covered the schoolyard, and it was here, in full view of a dozen or so other pupils that I started writing, but then found it was uncomfortable. The way the pen felt against the wall was awkward and the exercise book kept slipping down the wall. I stopped writing and put the exercise book back in my bag. Afterwards, I heard pupils in a group talking about it, many of whom knew my brother. They had seen me attempt to write out my homework with it pressed against the brick wall; before that I had tried doing it in other places, like on the ground near the wall.

'He did it on the wall,' became a good-natured joke amongst my brother's friends. They already knew my peculiarity and from my brother, understood it a bit better, but they were still embarrassed for me. I had wanted to do something but had not understood when and where it was appropriate. It was an act of impulse but my mind had not been conditioned to operate in the socially acceptable way and had also operated too fast.

The way the whole of the school functioned tended to be too fast for me to understand. A lot or pupils did their homework at school, but did it in a socially correct place, at a socially correct time.

I spent a lot of my time wandering round the school. When I was not wandering, I was running. I would have a lot of energy and would expend it through running round the buildings of the school. My brother told me I must have covered miles through running and walking, though I never tried to measure it. He told me I must be incredibly fit. I still laughed to myself, as I had always done, or grinned to myself when I thought of something amusing. Someone laughing and running at top speed must have made a sight. When a thought amused me, it amused me personally rather than anyone else.

There was an incident when I was younger when I had been in the car with my family, sitting in the back seat. We were travelling fast and I had been doing my usual thing of sticking my head outside the car window to feel the cold air sweep around my face and engulf it. I must have been grinning to myself very broadly as I often did, when another car passed us and a curly haired man with a beard stuck his head out and imitated my grin. There was another man beside him, driving. The way he had imitated me meant it was ridicule. This had made me want to stop doing what I did with my face. Putting my head out of the window as we sped along was a form of gratification to me, it was based on my own wishes. I did not consider how others might react, whether it was to sticking my head out of the window or grinning or both. There had been no precise consideration beforehand.

My family never objected to me sticking my head out. They may have got frustrated by it after a while but on the whole they were not all that aware of it. They allowed me to do something I enjoyed.

Most of the time the lessons at Springfield were bearable; if they were rowdy, I would hate it. If in turn the teachers were aggressive and shouted, I hated that too. There were some lessons full of energetic lads and lasses from Portsmouth that involved a lot of noise and shouting. I hated the disorder – the constant movement around the classroom, the chairs left around arranged sloppily. The boys would be standing in groups and the girls would be sitting talking to them.

The first form-tutor we had was a woman called Miss Pepper. I developed a crush on her that later changed into an appalling dislike. She was very strict. Maurice said I had a lateral, love/hate feeling for her. I was attracted to her but later started hating her.

Part of my personality, the autistic part, found it difficult to compare physical features with a person's characteristics. It was an over-idealistic outlook that could not reconcile attractive features to a harsh personality. To my autistic thinking, someone who dressed well and spoke well should have a pleasant personality and I was surprised when this was not the case.

Maths lessons were still as much a painful nuisance as they had always been. At Manor Court, I had found it so frustrating as I sat there trying to work it out that I would rock back and forth, as though I was trying to attack the problems – in a way, I suppose I was trying to do exactly that. I was the best-behaved boy in the class, compared to the others. We were the maths class set aside for the ones who were bad at maths. The teacher never commented on my bizarre behaviour to me because it never affected her, or disrupted the lesson; she only mentioned it once to my parents when she met them at a parents' evening meeting. After the meeting, my father told me she had told them that I got a 'bit mad' sometimes in her classroom. I had not cared what anyone thought because I had been too frustrated. I was more aware that I was acting bizarrely because I was in a focused situation, one that involved trying to do a certain thing.

In other situations, such as when I was roaming round the school, I was unfocused. When I was walking around, for example, I might pull a funny face or hug myself, or in most cases, take off running. I would be less aware of how odd I was acting.

The situation in the maths classroom involved me being physically focused by being seated, and mentally focused by trying to concentrate on the maths and sums that I found so hard. I was also socially focused, by having people around me in the classroom. My understanding of fractions and percentages has improved since then but that has been the limit.

I remember one maths teacher at middle school whom I literally drove to despair. I did not understand one particular sum. She had given up and just sat there at her desk, looking miserable. I kept trying to give her the right answer but she just said, 'No, William,' in a very tired voice.

Other kids had tried to help the situation by giving me what they thought was the right answer and I had tried repeating this to the teacher, but to no avail. There have been widely documented cases of autistic and Aspergic people being good at maths; in some cases, they have been mathematical geniuses.

I asked one college teacher, a lot later on, 'What is the secret of understanding maths?' She said it required the ability to understand a system that is based on processing and connecting factors related to numbers and statistics. I was and still am able to understand systems when they are applied to everyday living, like how people work in jobs, bus timetables, engines that run power stations; these I can understand because they serve a purpose. To me these aspects of everyday life form a system of communications. Maths, with its signs and numbers, has almost literally been a foreign language to me. I have only been able to understand it on a basic practical level, such as percentages.

Once, in my last few years at Springfield during a maths lesson, the class was asked a question about percentages. Like me, the class was made up of those in the lowest strata of mathematical understanding. We were asked by a teacher, 'Jack has £120. He spends fifty percent of it. How much has he got left?' The class gave different answers in turn.

When my turn came I said, 'Sixty pounds'; the others had all said fifty pounds.

The teacher announced, 'Do you know, only one of you got it right?' He then gave the correct answer of £60 and he looked at me and said, 'Aren't they stupid, William?'

While it was thought that low-functioning autistics were good at maths, low-functioning autistics tended to 'shut the world out' more than high-functioning ones. Because they are lower functioning socially and emotionally, it is possible they are less emotionally distracted than others and their thinking is more focused on a single subject. High-functioning autistics are often those with Asperger's Syndrome.

Another subject I was very bad at was woodwork. The teacher would show us what to do with a piece of wood in detail, such as chiselling bits out or making grooves. He would then send us away to get on with our own pieces. I would be back every few minutes to ask him about something I had missed, even though I had gone away thinking I could do it. When the teacher showed me how to do a practical piece of work in detail, I did not take it in, in the same detail.

'Mark it off, son,' the teacher said, referring to the marking of the piece of wood I had to carve out.

I would exasperate him, 'I've told you ten times!'

I had not been able to mentally observe something put together in detail. My eyes had seen him do it and my ears had heard him describe how to do it but I had not retained any of the instructions. Maybe he had done it too quickly and I needed to be shown several times? MDDB (Mentally deaf, dumb and blind) had prevented me processing and retrieving practical facts, to the extent that I just retained them.

Wood was a malleable substance (like clay) that was altered if given aggressive treatment with chisels and saws. The end product was things like chairs, shelves and boats. These did not appeal to me and were less exciting than what we made in metal work. Metal work was less complex but I could still get lost, still get MDDB and forget things.

In woodwork, I once nailed a piece of wood round the wrong way, in front of the whole class. They burst out laughing at the sight of the piece. I, unable to stop myself, started to cry. The woodwork teacher, being a kindly man, had taken the piece and after making the class leave, fixed it for me.

Metalwork seemed more practical because it had more power to connect things. Engines were made of metal and powered cars and planes; engines, cars and planes were all made of metal.

One subject where I almost always failed was French. My father kept reminding me of this when we tried to study for homework. I was told I failed to connect.

I could understand that the length and meaning of some French words could connect them to the English meaning. I could understand that, 'la' and 'un' were the same length as 'the' and 'an'. What I could not understand was the fact that the French word, 'regardez', and the English word, 'look' had the same meaning, but did not resemble each other.

My father would say, 'The trouble with you is you don't think, and you don't make connections.' In this case I did not make comparisons between the two words. The words, 'look' and 'regardez' both refer to social behaviour; they are both words describing social functioning.

The subjects I was good at were History, English and Classical Studies. History came under the heading of Humanities, which covered Religion, History and Cultural Studies. My Humanities teacher was called Miss Bentley. She gave me good reports for the subject, especially referring to what she described as 'oral work' and must have been referring to when I would mouth what I thought about what she had said. I would always be the first to give a view or observation about a subject she had lectured on in class. I remember her grinning with amusement when I said something that sounded highbrow and flowery.

One bad incident I remember was when we were all in a large class and had to copy something written on the board. I had been sitting there along with many other kids, writing it down. At the very end, ten minutes before the end of the lesson, I noticed a huge amount written up that I had not taken down. I furiously tried writing down as much as possible. At the time, I remember thinking, 'Had I not noticed all this? If I had not noticed, then why had I not noticed?'

The lesson ended before I could even try to get all the work done. We had to give in our exercise book to the table at the front of the class. Worried, I handed mine in to the pile. In form time the following day, my work was handed back to me by Miss Pepper. I opened it; what there was of my work had been unmarked. What was supposed to be there, but was not, had received the comments, 'Much too slow, much too slow. You must stop dreaming and start work.' This hurt and embarrassed me at the same time.

My lack of concentration was partly the reason for my bizarre behaviour outside the classroom. My dreaming embarrassed me but at the same time, I found it sacred. My daydreaming was not even what could be considered constructive daydreaming; none of my daydreams involved me. I would not imagine myself as a big hero in a film; I would only consider whoever was in the film. I cannot remember exactly what I dreamed about at school, only things I had made up about films and television.

Constructive daydreaming involves someone dreaming about something in a realistic context, such as one day being a father, who is head of a family. This was the dream of a man I once knew had confessed to having.

The problem was not what I was thinking about, but what I was not thinking about. I was thinking about lessons when they occurred; I would learn but I would not think about what was being taught. This had been a problem in French. In break time, I was never thinking about where I was, or who I was with.

Chapter 4

Meeting Others

*M*y parents had a boat we sometimes went sailing in. We would be sailing along in the water, all four of us sitting on the deck. My parents and my brother enjoyed it, my parents especially, inhaling the sea breeze and enjoying the sea. I would be bored and sit down reading a book. The sea only interested me when the waves from another passing boat or small ship would vibrate our boat, making it go up and down.

My parents were frustrated at my apparent lack of interest in sailing. They asked if I appreciated being in the boat itself. I could have put my book down, just to please them, but I did not sense other people's thoughts and feelings enough to do this, so I did not. They may have felt I did not actually enjoy being at sea; they were right at the time. If I was in that situation now, I would appreciate it more. I would spend hours at a time sitting and reading.

Other things that happened to me related to my family's hobby of sailing was that I once ran full-tilt into a cable. It was a steel cable that was winding a boat up the slipway at the sailing club we belonged to. I was in my usual state of running around when I ran into something hard and painful. The next second, someone was yelling at me, 'Get away, you stupid twit,' or words to that effect.

It was yelled by one of the two men working the crank.

My eyes filled with tears; I was firstly shaken by the physical experience of the cable and was now emotionally shaken by being yelled at so loudly and so harshly, and without warning. I wandered round the club for a while, feeling miserable, sobbing.

Another time at the sailing club, I was helping my father unload a dinghy down the slipway, we had it halfway on the pulley it was resting on.

'Right Bill, I want to go down.' The boat tilted on the pulley like a seesaw, with me at the other end of it. I was trying to understand what my father wanted. My mind now tried to focus as we had pulled the trailer down the slipway. I was still confused by what was going on. Trying to understand what I needed to do only made my confusion worse. I was trying to think quickly but without thinking at all.

My father had wanted to tilt his end of the boat down but I did not realise that this meant I had to push my end of the boat up, to compensate the seesaw action. Being MDDB prevented me understanding this.

I tried pulling my end of the boat down.

'No, no!' my father screamed. 'I want to go down, down.'

'It's embarrassing,' I cried out.

We must have looked like some sort of comedy act, one trying to go up while the other tried to go down.

I told my father I thought it was embarrassing for him to shout in a public place, to which he replied, 'Yes, it is embarrassing.' Later I think he tried to explain that I should have pushed the trailer up, but I was too confused to understand.

We would frequently sail to the Isle of Wight to stop at the Marina. I was hanging round the outskirts of the Quay when I had a stone thrown at me by one of a group of children. I asked him why he had done it.

'It's because you're queer, that's why.' Queer in this sense meant odd and unusual, rather than homosexual; it had its proper meaning back then.

I always knew that I was odd, but refused to believe that I was damaged or different from others. If I was different, I would like to think that I was different in the way all individuals are different; I felt hurt when another part of my mind considered me different by being dangerous, or inferior, or in constant social conflict with others. At the time, I regarded my feeling different as a form of individualism.

My father once asked me what I wanted to be when I grew up. I said I wanted to be an eccentric, partly to justify my different behaviour.

'Eccentrics have to earn their bread and butter,' my father had said. Eccentrics are people whose behaviour distances them from those with what is considered normal behaviour. Often they are consciously eccentric, which means they are aware of social norms but choose to ignore them. I behaved differently, not because I was aware of social norms and chose to ignore them but because I was not aware of normal social values and standards.

Sometimes, eccentrics are seen as happy in their defiance, as having a sort of 'celebrated individualism'. A person who is seen to defy social convention because they are not aware of social convention, can himself or herself, be anything but happy.

When my father had asked me what I wanted to do, he had meant what did I want to do for a living.

Most of my spare time was spent at home in the evenings, watching television, reading, doing homework and going for walks. I would feel blank, wandering round Courmount Grove, and the roads surrounding it. I would always walk round that area of Cosham, as it was the area nearest to our house; it may have been an autistic resistance to change. It was sameness that I always wanted, a fixed habit and pattern of behaviour. I never ventured all that far from our house to areas surrounding Drayton, the local shopping centre.

I was twelve when I first experienced feelings of impulse and initiative but did not respond to them. I feared if I started doing things, I would have to face the fact that I had not done them earlier. I mentioned this to my father. He did not explain to me that this was an odd thing to think because he did not know the proper thing to say. He did not reason with me about my attitude, he just said, 'Oh, you'll be alright,' meaning that nothing bad would happen to me. If I had said the same thing to some other people, they might be dumbfounded, because it would not have made sense.

I had not realised that having an interest would have therapeutic benefits. It may have been general timidity, combined with a possible fear of people that stopped me pursuing an interest. I could not judge the views of others, whether they would approve or disapprove of my actions. I knew that some things I did might seem odd but was unable to be objective in the way I viewed my own actions.

At school, during dinnertime, I would inevitably wander down to the school youth club and this would occasionally happen at break time as well; I had wandered in there on my first day and had my bag thrown in my face. The youth club was located in one corner of the school. I was taunted and teased at the club more than anywhere else. When I complained of this to my family, my brother mentioned that all the 'erks' congregated round that area; 'erks' were the school layabouts.

The youth club attracted me because of the music that was played. It emitted from a jukebox at the far end of the building.

It was disco music from the charts, the sort I liked at the time. The main building of the youth club was darkly lit and the only people who danced were the girls. I would constantly roam from one spot in the youth club to another. I did not get up and dance to the music because something inside told me that doing so would invite ridicule; even with my level of social understanding I knew that dancing in the middle of the floor would look odd.

The music made me restless and I think I was once asked by one of the girls why I wandered around so much.

'The music stimulates me,' I had replied.

'The music stimulates him,' the girl had repeated to her friend.

The music may have had an effect on my autistic senses; autistic people might crave more stimuli than a non-autistic person. I had always enjoyed disco music that had a good beat and a dramatic sounding melody. Any of the right music containing drama and irony can stimulate my emotions.

One unusual habit I developed in the youth club was when I felt bored and restless, as I often did in the youth club, I would go around picking up litter off the club floor and put it in the bin. This of course, attracted comments from other pupils. They called me a 'Womble', after the TV puppets that went around picking up litter from Wimbledon Common. One boy in the club attacked me verbally. The fact that he was smaller than me, thus more vulnerable to me than I was to him, did not embarrass me. When I told my parents about this, they felt it was silly that I should be bullied by someone smaller than me; they understood the social implications better than I did.

The smaller lad may have just been imitating the comments of the other pupils, since he later turned out to be a perfectly pleasant person. At the time, he just seemed upsetting. My mind was not socially cognitive to see through outward impressions and appearances.

On one occasion I got fed up and gave him a glancing blow on the head. It was as he was entering school.

'And you'll get more,' I shouted after him. He eventually drifted away from me.

My brother constantly complained that I did not have any focused relationships with other pupils. He said that he himself would go to a spot at the school and talk to a group of friends he had. He talked about occasions when someone would say, 'Hello, William,' to me as I passed and I would totally ignore them. There was a time I was in a toilet when a group of boys asked me what I had done during the holidays. Slowly and awkwardly, I explained how I had gone somewhere with my family. It was forced and stilted. I did not know how they would react to what I was saying. When I left the toilet, I heard laughter from behind the door. They boys were not being malicious; they just could not help themselves.

As I walked, or raced round the school being MDDB, it became difficult for me to distinguish how people reacted. It was difficult anyway, but passing so many people so quickly I could not distinguish between the 'Alrights' and the 'Hellos' that were called out to me. It seemed half of the school knew me, but I did not know them, individually at any rate. They were young, fast and spoke in different accents. In my early stage of social understanding, I tended to judge people according to what they were, rather than who they were.

Maurice Bridgeland, on discussing this with me, had said that going up to another pupil and saying, 'Alright', was another way of saying, 'Hello, how are you?' which could begin a social relationship. If the person addressed replied, 'Yeah, I'm alright. You alright?' this would be a continuation of social interaction.

This period of time was the very beginning of any social understanding on my part. I liked discussing heavy subjects, as I still do now but Maurice told me I could perhaps begin on a very simple level with small things, such as greetings.

All, if not most, of the pupils seemed surly to me – I was timid enough in my MDDB state of being. I found it difficult to prepare to meet people as I knew I would not be able to evaluate them properly. There were however, many people I could talk to in lessons and elsewhere.

One bloke said hello to me on one occasion; I was going to say hello back, but then he gave a funny look to his friend, so I remained mute and blocked them both out. On another occasion the same boy had got hold of my arm and swung me round when I was passing him in the corridor. 'Hello, Will,' he said and introduced me to his friends. He had done this to force a reaction from me as he thought I'd snubbed him earlier. He wanted me to talk to him and his friends. We became good social contacts; I had no real friends then.

I did not communicate much with my brother at school, he was older than me, in a different year and as a result I was in none of his classes. He told me that I acted as though I was socially superior to other pupils, or a 'cut above' them when he had seen me round the school.

There was one boy I wanted to be friendly with. He was new to the school and his name was Andy Conliffe. I wanted to be his friend because he was so well spoken. I liked well spoken, sensitive seeming people because they posed less of a social threat to me. Andy Conliffe had come from a boarding school and was invited to talk to the whole class about his experiences there. He seemed open and friendly when he talked.

I would try speaking to him about the things I liked talking about. I once asked him what he thought about Northern Ireland.

'What about Northern Ireland?' he responded impatiently.

He went abroad to the United States and Canada. I asked him why the Americans seemed to like *Monty Python*; for some reason I was obsessed with America and the Americans. It may have come from a time when my mother bought me a book about the Wild West. Maurice said it had something to do with America being so powerful and me feeling so timid, plus other reasons that I don't remember now.

In reply to my *Monty Python* question, Andy told me it was because they liked sarcasm. He then went on to say that Americans were very sarcastic people and continued with a crass, foul-mouthed, anti-American statement that repelled me.

I asked him what Canadians were like.

'Well,' began Conliffe in what he imagined to be a Canadian accent. 'They talk in Canadian accents,' he drawled. It was only later that I realised what these comments were meant to express. Another favourite trick of his was to pretend that he could not hear me.

'What?' he would say, turning his ear to me as though straining to hear. I would repeat myself.

'What?' he would say. 'What?' he would say again, 'I can't hear you Bill.' This would go on in the school classroom during break.

Eventually, I once asked him, 'Do I bore you Andy?'

He looked at me very wearily and said, 'Probably, Wilber.'

My lack of social understanding had prevented me from assessing him quickly enough. I desired to connect with someone who I thought would provide me with profound conversation but I had not read any of the social signs. I had

had an inkling that Andy Conliffe did not really want to talk to me. If he did want to talk to someone, it was about what he wanted to talk about – in his case, sport; he had once told me this. I would later learn that it was all right for me to talk about what I wanted to talk about in situations like this, providing I did not do it too much. I also learnt that this applied to other people as well, not just me. The best solution is to balance topics of conversation.

Girls still teased me; sometimes it was spiteful, other times it was playful. In one particular case it was about sexual feelings rather than anything more extensive, like sexual activity or foreplay; I was hardly very advanced in social and sexual relationships and some girls picked up on this. I perceived any sexual advance made to me by a girl as some sort of attack. I hated any direct sexual reference because it seemed dirty and it embarrassed me.

In metalwork, a girl stroked my chin. I struck her. The teacher who saw this told me if she bothered me again I should tell him. If a man had stroked a girl's chin then or in the present social climate, it would be considered far more serious. Social relationships are very complex, and changes in society can often change their social implications.

Another time, a girl came alongside me as I walked home from school. We had just passed through the school gates as she came to within an inch of me, as we were progressing at the same speed. She was grinning and getting too close, so I punched her in the eye, not too hard. She rejoined her friend with her hand over her eye and I heard her friend say, 'I told you so!'

The worst incident of all occurred when I was in the youth club. The youth club had a languid, squalid image that as my brother had said, could only attract the 'erks'. I was standing at one end of the building with my back to the wall. Through the window of the wall opposite, two boys, who were younger than me, had made faces at me. I had gone outside to find them, only to have them disappear. I returned to standing in the youth club but they returned to make more childish faces through the window. They then disappeared again. I felt strung up and frustrated. A short while later, I noticed a girl, leaning against a radiator that was attached to the wall. She had a languid look in her eyes that were for a moment, focused on me. The boys' teasing had been the last straw and I found myself walking over to the girl in a few long strides, reaching up, grabbing hold of her hair and pulling her off the radiator. She screeched as she fell to the floor and sat there outraged.

She exclaimed, 'What the hell did you do that for?' Or words to that effect. I was still angry and responded with strong words.

'I don't have to take it from you. I've been taking it for years from people like you. I've had enough of your rubbish,' I shouted, then stormed out of the building. It had been a flash of temper.

As I walked round the school I eventually cooled off. It was then I realised what I had done as I saw the girl talking to two teachers; I began to cry. I sat outside the Head's office almost in hysterics, and in floods of tears. Eventually, I was brought into the Deputy Head's office; the girl was already in there.

The Deputy Head ranted at me, 'There was no need to blow up like that. There was no need to attack somebody. Perhaps you need to apologise.' I apologised to the girl. The Deputy Head raged at me the way he had raged at the group of boys on my first day. I was in tears and blubbering too much to be scared of him shouting. The fact he was shouting did not make any difference anyway; I had endured a huge amount of social pressure from, as I felt, being attacked socially. This occurred all the time I was at Springfield. It was like a wall that surrounded me and mocked me; it was something I eventually attacked with my fists and in this case, it was an innocent girl who suffered. Later I was far better equipped to deal with social teasing, often by ignoring it.

Maurice would have put it down to a lack of social understanding; this was what I would later do.

'You can't attack someone just for looking at you,' one of the teachers told me after the girl had talked to her. I had told the teacher that I had attacked her because she looked at me in a funny way.

The girl continued being outraged, 'You shouldn't be in this school!' She thought I was somehow abnormal because my behaviour had seemed abnormal. I had not been sent to Cliffdale; if I had, I would not be at Springfield. My behaviour before now had not been violent, only odd and I had been the subject of violence previously, rather than the perpetrator.

The Deputy Head told me I would have to be punished, but I was not. I was told to leave the office while he spoke to the girl. I overheard him talking to the girl in an earnest manner; he may have been explaining my past problems to her, that he was more than aware of.

In lessons I would sometimes show a lack of social understanding, which would manifest itself at various levels and in various ways. I would be arrogant in my attitude to other children while being timid in my response to them.

The Humanities class was particularly rowdy and I hated it. In between the teacher trying to keep order, I tried to help her by telling students to be quiet. The students' reaction was predictably hostile.

'Piss off, Furlong.'

'What's it to you, Furlong?'

'Want to meet me outside?'

We had a slide show in another lesson. I described one slide in a very intellectual, flowery way so the next student to speak described me in sarcastic terms, as 'Professor Furlong'. This got applause from the rest of the class.

My lack of self-realisation also manifested itself in a French lesson where we had to describe each other. It was an exercise in communication where we described what we looked like to the student next to us. My inability, together with the inability of some other students to describe themselves, made the French teacher angry.

'At your age, you should know what you look like,' she snapped. I had understood what she meant but did not fully comprehend or understand its implications in relation to maturity.

In form session, I was asked how old I was.

'I'm fourteen, I think,' I had replied. The teacher looked at me for a long time, and then gave me an amused smile.

'You know how old you are, don't you William?'

There is an age when a child starts to keep track of how old they are, year by year. I had not started to keep track of mine.

Chapter 5

Other interests

*I*n my free time, I went to the local library; I had also started going to the central library in Commercial Road, which was far bigger. I would walk in and read about subjects that interested me such as history, war and politics. On one particular visit, I asked the librarian if they had any books about Korea.

'Careers, yes. We should have something about them,' she said, walking to another shelf.

'No, I mean Korea, the country.' I was not planning for the future or thinking about it; I was in my own world, in more ways than one. It was the world of history and international affairs. The rest of the real world seemed to close in on me and this closing in on me made me angry.

The school's Christmas disco came up and I went to attend it. It was held at the youth club and was full of children, jostling with each other. I felt agitated as I was dancing; I had been agitated all day. There was a lot of movement and light and noise around. I began to feel angry with Americans because they were always so confident; anyone can have prejudices. Later Maurice said that it was not just Americans I hated, but people generally. I was so angry with everybody else for being able to do things easily that I tended to focus my anger on particular groups of individuals because I had no understanding of the world. It was this, combined with the constant feed of American TV programmes and films that I kept seeing. I had watched so much television it had filled the part of my mind that did not recognise fact.

'It is the greatest tragedy that all we know about America is from films and television,' my father had once said. It is a sentiment I agree with now, but did not recognise at the time. I could not separate fiction from everyday life, reality from fantasy. My lack of understanding of the world was due to my inability to see it in a structured state. That America was three thousand miles away and not connected to Portsmouth; Portsmouth is in the south of England, England is part of Great Britain, were all connections that I did not see.

I stormed out of the disco and proceeded home. I walked angrily all the way from the youth club through the school, all the way up the alleyway leading to Drayton. I walked all the way to my parents' house. I went up to the front door, threw it open, entered and then slammed the door behind me.

'I'm going to kill an American,' I bellowed. I realised later that this sort of behaviour could make me certifiable, something my father would later discuss with me.

My parents were in the living room. They were perturbed by me slamming the door and shouting; they were expecting me back but not so abruptly. I had had tantrums before about Americans, which had also upset my parents. On this occasion it was more serious.

'I'm going to find an American tourist, find out where he is staying and stick a knife in this throat as he's sleeping,' I had growled, on entering the living room. I had sat down, put the TV on and started to watch; oblivious to a lot of the consternation I had just sparked off.

'But Bill,' my mother cried, 'that's murder. They'll put you in prison, can't you see that? You'll go to prison, there will be a trial, then you'll go to prison for life. Think what that would do to us.' She was right of course, I had not realised the implications of what I was saying; it had caused a lot of consternation to my parents by saying it.

Sometimes a person can experiment with what they say to somebody as a sort of game. They might say something to offend or anger, not out of malice but to get a reaction. I was not consciously experimenting with my parents. My statement did not strike me as immoral because it mentioned killing, also it did not strike me as bizarre because it involved a particular group I had experienced very little, if any, contact with. It was simply my own feelings erupting after being pent up for such a long time; it was partly my inability to communicate with others and experiment that was making me so frustrated.

I had expressed my feelings, now it was my mother's turn to express hers. She brought her hand down on the chair; I was sitting on the armrest.

'You've never paid any attention to what's around you. It's always been going for walks, watching television and going to the library,' she wailed. I had rarely considered or questioned the things my mother mentioned. I had little impulse to not go to the library or not go for walks, and least of all, to not watch television. The autistic mind demands sameness, a constant routine and a constant set of habits. These are what I had created, and these are what I had fallen into.

I calmed down, after much arguing.

'Don't worry,' my mother remarked sarcastically, 'if you do kill an American, Bill, we'll always visit you when you're in prison.'

I had been, and still am, very inhibited socially – that is one of the things autism is, ultimate social inhibition. That night at the disco however, I was less inhibited and had broken out in the worst possible way.

Later that night, when we were all in bed, I broke out again, shouting. My mother broke down standing there in my bedroom; my father was also standing in the bedroom. He said he wanted to speak to me alone and ushered my mother out of the room whilst he knelt besides my bed, 'All this, about you wanting to kill an American and all this wanting to sneak into his hotel room and slit his throat, it's upsetting your mother.' He went on, calmly and reasonably, 'Do you think....,' very slowly and carefully. 'Do you think....,' he repeated. Then came the reason dad had sent mum from the room, 'that you're going mad?'

The idea of madness did not especially scare me. I had behaved in a bizarre way, but did not understand the implications of the term, 'mad'. If autism is a form of madness, then I was mad anyway, being autistic. I had once recognised one implication of madness – that madness was something of the world and a fact of everyday society. This meant that I had recognised its implications but I had not retained the knowledge. I had forgotten it.

I later realised the strain and confusion that causes madness, that madness is sometimes connected with violence. In this case, I had threatened violence. I now recognise violence as a form of evil, which can enter some emotional and behavioural states that are considered to constitute madness. It is an evil that strikes not just the person perceived as mad, but potentially endangers others as well. That night I had attacked and hurt my parents emotionally by causing them consternation. In other cases, when a person shouts, screams and yells in a tantrum, it only causes discomfort to others.

The first thing I did was go and see Maurice. I had made an

appointment with him and went into his office as usual.

'I keep getting frequent attacks of anti-Americanism,' I told him. Maurice seemed puzzled.

'Well that's not rare, a lot of people say that they don't like Americans but when they are questioned and asked if they don't like all Americans, they say....'

'I want to kill an American,' I said, interrupting him. Maurice was dumbstruck. We talked it over and it eventually passed.

That same year I considered joining the Army, I say considered because it came as a thought, an impulsive subconscious thought. It may have been inspired by a TV programme I saw called *Spearhead*. I had watched so much television for such a long time that it had come to dominate me. My brother once told me that all I knew about life was from what I had seen on television. He told me I had no concept of life and that television was just rubbish. I was sixteen when he said it. The programme *Spearhead* had portrayed soldiers as being uncouth, frequently crude, loud and aggressive. All things that for a long time had scared me.

I mentioned that I was considering joining the Army to my parents and they had discussed it with me. It concerned me that they were taking it seriously; one half of my mind wanted me to join this organisation that scared me and was full of frightening men, whilst the other half was too scared to join. My parents posed questions and made statements like: 'Could you kill someone on the battlefield?', 'You'd be with a lot of other men all the time,' and, 'I wouldn't want you being sent to Northern Ireland,' which came from my mother.

I had considered joining up exactly because it was something that scared me and was full of men I considered frightening. My feelings however, were inspired by something fictitious, which may or may not have directly reflected reality. The Army was an organisation that represented reality and hardship in its most austere form; I wanted subconsciously to be woken up. I wanted me to take on my MDDB self and fight him.

My father suggested I join the Army Cadets since I was too young to joining the regular army. In the end we decided I was too sensitive to join.

Maurice had asked me questions such as what would I do if I was the only person left on earth. These were questions designed to test my response to the challenge of physical reality – at the time I had no idea of this reality. What I knew of it seemed grim and depressing.

I had been seeing Maurice Bridgeland for the past three years; he was a child psychologist and thus a therapist. I had been seeing Maurice for a long time but still had not achieved any dramatic results as yet. He knew about my problem because he had diagnosed it.

I did not understand about instrumental attitude involving an instrumental course of action. An instrumental course of action was one that sought to change a personality. It would change their behaviour and their personality by placing them in an other person's situation, or else submitting them to a particular experience. A more common term to apply to what can affect a person's state is therapeutic. Both therapeutic and instrumental refer to the objective of changing or improving a person. This is mainly practised in the area of therapy called psychoanalysis.

I was still behaving strangely round the house and my family were still pointing it out to me. My father once saw me making one of my ducking movements with my body. He commented, 'That's why they make fun of you at school.'

'It'll be alright when I'm older, dad,' I replied. My reply sounded naïve and reflected a naïve view of the world that wanted stability and thought that the world beyond school would be perfect. My idea of mature behaviour meant behaving in an ordered manner in class; I would later redefine my concept of maturity. Maturity could be defined in the dictionary as growth and development, which could be mental, physical and emotional. I myself had achieved very little social growth and thus very little social maturity. I was the social equivalent of a new born, or even unborn, child.

'I wouldn't be too sure about when you're older, Bill. People might be cruel to you.' My father ascertained that people are cruel. 'They might even be cruel to you at work; they'll probably call you the ducking mule.' The ducking mule was a piece of machinery whose action compared with my own ducking movement. It made me a bit worried, if not slightly taken aback.

The next time I saw Maurice, I posed the question of whether people would tease me and be unkind to me when I went to work because of the way I acted.

'That would depend on the sort of people you were with, Bill.' He paused, then began the first step towards one of the most significant aspects of my condition. 'You see Bill, you don't know how other people work.' When he said this he had probably been thinking of how my behaviour seemed to other people, and how my behaviour, such as my ducking habit, seemed in areas such as a work situation. Seeming odd in a work situation was the context I had brought up but Maurice widened it to include a greater number of different contexts. He gave me the example of when I had been in church one Sunday morning and the vicar had given a sermon. Afterwards, I had complimented the vicar on what I thought was a lovely sermon; my mother and Maurice had been there with me. Maurice told me that the way I complimented the vicar was not really done. There were no real rules, only that praising a sermon gave the impression that it was being judged in a critical light. All my behaviour was conditioned by what I didn't think rather than what I did think.

I knew I viewed everything from my own perspective and from within my own feelings. My father sometimes told me I was selfish and too introspective; I did not pass cups through the hatch into the kitchen to be washed; I did not talk to my family enough.

For a brief period I attended a youth club for physically handicapped as well as able-bodied people in Portsmouth. I had almost befriended a blind bloke from there and was going to play chess with him but I spent most of my time dancing to the club's music. I left after an incident with a boy in a wheelchair. I had been dancing when I decided to take a breather. Just before I sat down the boy said, 'Like your dancing. Can I fuck you?' I had been naturally responding to my own impulse to dance on the floor. It was a combination of my love of music with a certain amount of energy. I did realise that I might look odd to other people but had not wanted to respond to what I realised. When the insult came, I had been half expecting it. I was used to being insulted but had not yet learnt to think of insults and social attacks as opportunities for social contact. I could have turned a situation round by using it as a starting point for a relationship.

My reply to the remark, 'Like your dancing. Can I fuck you?' could have been, 'No, but you can dance with someone,' or 'Sorry, you're not my type,' or 'Oi, that's enough!'

In reality, I should have stopped dancing or danced no more than anyone else; I had not judged the situation. I was afraid of being teased and taunted and this restricted me socially. I could have used the boy's reaction to learn from my mistake and then could have made friends elsewhere in the club. There were many other people at the club but my reasoning dealt in absolutes, which made me afraid of a group of people or in this case, a club full of people because I was afraid of just one person.

Another attempt was made to involve me with people. This was through a rambling club and it turned out to be the biggest disaster of them all. I had been told that a lot of the ramblers were far older than me; this had not deterred me.

I was picked up at one of the member's house. Together with twenty to thirty other people, all aged in their sixties and seventies, I went for walks in different parts of Hampshire every Sunday. We would stop for our packed lunch after walking a certain distance. It was during one of these lunch breaks on the sixth or seventh ramble with them that one of the ramblers commented, 'I want to be alone.' This was a quote from Greta Garbo, and it was said about me.

The fellow who said it was a gentleman in his sixties. He was sitting with a group of other ramblers against some trees. 'I want to be alone,' he repeated. He then told me I very rarely talked to the others; I walked on my own and read the paper. The only time I had properly started talking to one of them was after reading an article about the Royal Horse Artillery. Even discussing that had seemed distant to me, as though I was only talking about what I had wanted to talk about. This was the problem I had, I had not got used to small talk; I always wanted to get on to the broad, large issues such as politics and history and a lot of intelligent matters.

There came an occasion one Sunday. The group stopped to have lunch at a café cum resting place. It was in a clearing in one of the Hampshire woods. There was another group sitting on the same bench as us, along with a lot of other people. I had just finished my cake and sandwich when I saw a large number of people get up and move out. I did likewise, going off with this group of people I thought were my group of ramblers. It was an hour later when one of them, a lady, asked me if I was one of her group. She asked some of the others if I was one of the group; apparently they did not know me. This was another rambling club that I had accidently gone off with. They were befuddled as to what to do with me. They asked each other if there was any way they could contact my original group, or if I could get back to Portsmouth on my own. They suggested a train from Petersfield to Portsmouth; I mentioned I felt more familiar with buses.

Eventually my original group found me. The other group took me to a point where the original group came and collected me. I had dreaded the reception I would get. The van we travelled in drew up and the group's leader got out, 'Where have you been? You got lost,' she started. She was an elderly lady who sounded both angry and concerned.

I got into the van to take me back. There were two other elderly ramblers sitting there who were annoyed and told me of the trouble I had caused. I must have been late because my parents were concerned as well. My mother told me she had received a phone call from the leader of the ramblers who had said that I was not mentally with any of the other ramblers, that I did not talk to any of the other group and ran ahead. My parents, especially my father, were baffled by what had happened; this was at first. Over Sunday tea, my father had become furious, 'How could you get lost, for God's sake?'

I was embarrassed, but had wanted to get over it. 'Why are you upset?' I asked.

'Because quite frankly, I'm a bit ashamed,' he replied. 'I wouldn't have minded you being with a group of boys wandering around Cosham and ending up on Southampton Hill, providing you weren't involved in any crime. You're selfish,' he bellowed at me across the table. A piece of meat flew out of his mouth, narrowly missing me. He had been eating and unable to control himself.

There had been many other times when he got angry and told me I was selfish. He told me it wasn't so much a moral issue as a social issue for me. He thought it was selfish of me not to have any friends or not be responsive enough to others. All he had said about me going around with a group of boys and having fun with them and companionship; they were the things that deep down I had always wanted. I had wanted friends on and off, but it was something that seemed like gold to me at the top of a hundred foot cliff-top. I had really needed to select the right sort of friends. I was now too old to have the sort of friends my father talked about – the opportunity to have a truly gregarious relationship with a group of mates had existed when I was eleven or twelve. That had now passed.

Chapter 6

Going on 16

*I*discovered at this age that I needed glasses to watch television. My father had a theory that introverted people tended to be more short-sighted than extroverted people. I did not like wearing them. I may have had the subconscious feeling, common amongst kids that wear glasses, that to wear them was odd and demeaning.

I was now in the fifth form of school and doing 'O' levels. I was showing more interest in my fellow students because we were in smaller groups and it was easier to talk to them. I did not swear as much as they did. I once did swear and they were taken aback by it because it was out of character. I tried to make friends with some of them and would hear about them meeting after school and having parties; they probably went to pubs and nightclubs in their spare time. I was too concerned with study to ever attempting these things.

I had always found study more frustrating than other students; I would read a piece of work and try to remember it word for word, because that's what I thought studying was. It was only later when I began to show an active interest in the subject concerned that I learnt around the subject, which helped me to study.

I could learn about specific things as well as think of them; one of these was the situation in El Salvador. This was in 1980 and part of my interest in world affairs. I was not however attuned to a more general understanding that reflected a world view. At the time, I did not have a world view.

Some girls made cruel fun of my lack of social range and my inability to make friends. They pretended to invite me round to a place for sex. Luckily, I spoke to Maurice, who advised me against going. Thus I saved myself from this social embarrassment.

I was in two halves when it came to making friends; half of me wanted to make friends, the other half did not. It can depend on what part of an autistic person's personality is socially withdrawn. Is the person withdrawn because they are autistic, or does being autistic make the person's entire behaviour and personality withdrawn? The real issue might be whether autism is part of an individual's personality per se, or alien to it. Can a person be withdrawn in their nature, as well as autistic?

One social activity I took part in was the school play; I played Philostrate in 'A Midsummer Night's Dream.' I was told I had to project my voice more.

Being bullied at Springfield had come to a head. A local character had gone too far and he did not even go to the school anymore. He was a bully in every sense of what could be called a bully. He was bigger than me and a lot of other people, and he would act mean. He was also as thick as two planks; an ex-pupil who would taunt me as I passed the school gates.

I managed to ignore all this until one Tuesday afternoon. I was emerging from a newsagent's in Cosham when he punched me slightly in the stomach; I went home crying. I was distraught that this had happened; it seemed to be the price I paid for refusing to have friends and refusing to conform. Being physically abused was different though; it had confronted me with physical reality.

Later, I told my parents that if I saw the boy again I was prepared to fight him. A few days later I did see the bully at his usual place – at the school gates. I was tensed up and scared but determined. He saw me and screamed, 'Willieeeeee,' as he normally would. I ran at him with both fists held out. He ran away and I chased him, we went round the area surrounding the school entrance and the bike shed. Then I gave up; he could run faster than me.

The next week I saw him and the same thing happened. I was chasing him around the same area when he turned his head and snapped, 'What are you chasing me for, you cunt? I can run faster than you, see.' He stopped, we wrestled for a while before a caretaker broke us up and sent us in separate directions.

I was walking home when my tormentor caught up with me and demanded I explain why I kept chasing him. This was especially scary in view of the fact that I could not beat him up.

'You keep swearing at me,' I said, as he walked alongside me.

'And?' he demanded.

'You punched me coming out of the shop.'

'That was only a little tap,' he claimed. He threatened that if I didn't stop chasing him, he would stop forgetting this was just a laugh and give me a real fight. He stopped swearing at me but instead started giving me funny looks. Eventually he started greeting me in a friendly way. The incident helped to teach me that a bad relationship could be better than no relationship at all; being punched in the chest in the shop had helped 'wake me up' to a certain degree.

In between the confrontation with the bully and him eventually becoming friendly, I became very low. It was the first time I had experienced emotional disturbance. The disturbance took the form of being sick in the mornings, lack of sleep and frequent weariness. I even considered suicide.

When I confessed to Maurice, he told me of the effect it would have on my family and others. He encouraged me to write a note expressing my feelings and what they might lead to. However, he warned me about not letting my family see it. I wrote out the note and took it to him. Maurice read out to me what I had written, exploring the implications and explaining them to me. This helped my suicidal period pass.

Around this time, my mother took me to a CND meeting; it was the early 80s and the anti-nuclear movement was in full swing. My mother had become associated with the campaign for nuclear disarmament through some Quaker friend of hers. I attended a few CND parties and met a man called Mike Tracey at one. Mike Tracey invited me to his flat for dinner with his roommates. A week later Mike, myself and the same roommates went for a walk in the country. Mike was twice my age at thirty-two, but was now my first friend outside my family. He was the first person outside school that I had established a proper relationship with. I now had someone I could go places and do things with. He was invited to my sixteenth birthday party. This was the last time I saw him; afterwards we drifted apart.

'Have you any friends your own age, Bill?' my brother asked.

'No,' I replied, rather upset.

In the class for General Studies, I could always be counted on by the teacher to start a debate or give my opinion. I must have seemed a bit detached to the other twenty or so students, crowded into the common room. I would make statement after statement; I talked about what I enjoyed talking about, oblivious to whether the others enjoyed it or not.

I left school after attempting two 'O' levels.

'You have gained more confidence, haven't you Bill?' was the last thing the head of the fifth form enquired, before I left. I suppose what he would miss was the way I spoke up in General Studies. The General Studies lessons had covered such topics as unemployment, Northern Ireland and general politics. I was very interested in these subjects. Maurice said that in our discussions, I was more concerned about the world's problems than about my own.

Chapter 6

Social Cognition

*T*he plan was to send me to South Downs College. It was hoped I would get the 'O' levels I had failed to get at school. Earlier that year, between college and school, my father took me down to the employment centre at the bottom of Cosham High Street. We had pulled up in front of the employment centre in my dad's white car. I was about to get out when I asked about the door locks securing the car door. I mumbled something like, 'How do you work them? Do they go up or down?' My father looked at me with an expression that was sad, angry and disappointed. We sat there for several seconds before he spoke.

I was sixteen years old and could not work out how to operate the locks on a car door. I had been fiddling with one – up and down before leaving it on 'up'. After what seemed an eternity, my father started to get out.

'Come on,' he said.

We proceeded up the stairs to see the people in charge. My father was dead silent. We stopped outside an office and sat waiting to be called.

I started to say something. 'Oh, assholes!' my father snapped, cutting me off. He was angry the way he got angry with children at school; I knew why he was angry.

I was called in to see the careers advisor; there was a man

and a woman. The man had been reading through my file.

'You're 'socially autistic',' he told me. This meant, in other words, high-functioning autistic. If they had witnessed what just happened in the car, they would have had a clear demonstration of it. They asked me if I had ever had any experience of part time work. I said that I had not.

'Then you've never had any experience of a work situation?' the woman, quite rightly pointed out.

It was true that I did not know the concept of work experience – I did not even know the concept of work. I thought it was something I was supposed to do because everyone else did it. Previously, I understood it as the basic way human beings supported themselves, by buying food and other things. This knowledge had not kept in my mind though. I had told Maurice I would be satisfied when one day I was living in a village with a wife, had an office job and a place to commute to every morning. Maurice asked me what village in Portsmouth I envisaged living in? I told him I did not know. I had no concept of factual reality, this was a reality of time, space and personal effort. The wishes I expressed to Maurice were for stability. This was during the time I was being bullied and attacked by other kids. My being punched just outside the newsagent had brought the whole thing to a climax and caused me to make the statement to Maurice, as I wanted some stability.

I left the interview and the careers centre with the intention of finding part time work. I planned to do this whilst studying – it was what the centre had advised. My father and I drove home from Cosham in complete silence.

When we got home, my father began, 'You would have been better of if you'd just admitted,' he had a solemn expression as he stood half way up the stairs, 'that you've never paid any attention to how things work, or what people are doing, or what's going on around you.' He was referring to the door lock incident.

It is interesting to consider how other fathers might have reacted. If my father had said, 'You're acting as though you're stupid by not being able to work out how to open a door lock,' I would still not have been able to understand the concept. I was too young, and had not reached the right stage of development.

I told people about how my father told me I was not aware of what was around me. They just dismissed it in so many words; they scoffed at it.

At an earlier age, I was not mature enough for my parents to discuss it with me as I was unaware that I was unaware. If they had tried comparing my lack of mental awareness with my general high level of intelligence, I would have been baffled. I was still MDDB and was still not aware of what other people were thinking. All I knew about what my father was thinking was that he was angry about my 'lack of awareness'. My father, and to a certain extent my mother, did not fully understand one of my main problems. Anymore than I did.

I have now come to understand what is supposed to be my core problem, but back then I had far less understanding of it and its implications.

I once related to my father what Maurice had told me, in the way Maurice had described it about not knowing how people work. My father seemed to understand and replied, 'Oh you don't know how other people think and function? I could have told you that.'

Many years later, I had a broader understanding because I had a broader range of examples and experiences to draw from. I still did not discuss them with my father.

How many people, I wonder, can understand the

subject of social understanding? Most people understand it subconsciously and innately, so it is not a problem to them. How many people, statistically or otherwise, can understand that social understanding can be a problem to some people? A problem that becomes a central issue in their lives?

My lack of social understanding had been in evidence with my family as much as with anyone else. When I had begun my 'little acts', as my mother called them, I danced round the kitchen and in other rooms in the house. My brother told me at the time that I might be judged as insane and put away.

One time, I was going out swimming with a group of people and we needed to catch a bus.

'Don't let any of the girls pay for your fare,' my father had said, as he drove me to the bus stop.

'Social cognitive', if it had been around at the time, would have said, 'It's true, men are supposed to pay for themselves, and women if they like, but women are not supposed to pay for men.' This was social information that social cognitive would have processed in this situation. Social cognitive would emerge much later on in my life as a useful function that helped me to understand socially acceptable behaviour.

I had always known there was something wrong with me but did not know exactly what; I was extremely vague to myself about it. I knew I seemed odd to other people but did not know how to appear more normal. I did not understand the broader implications of my 'little acts' or what others might think of them. Was I actually mad because I knew it was not the done thing to make others think I was mad, but did it anyway? Or am I completely sane because I realise all that and do know what I am doing? That is one irony of the autistic condition.

I did not think of myself as autistic; it is an ugly word to me, even though I have come to accept it more. I was not confident and lacked the preparation and emotional fortification to become confident. The instrumental system for this was lacking.

I went through a period when I would actually admit to myself that I was not confident.

I was in our front garden one time when I shouted up to my brother who was in the top bedroom, 'I'm not confident!'

At first my brother could not answer, he did not know how to help me.

'In what way?' my brother replied dumbly.

'I haven't got any friends,' I replied. I had repeated this to Maurice Bridgeland and he told me I had my family as friends. I had Maurice himself as a friend and I had Mike Tracey as a friend, that was 'til we drifted apart. There were other people that I knew; the trouble was that they were friends of my mother's who were far older than me. I had not made and built on any relationships with people my own age.

After I told Maurice this, he surmised, 'What you mean is you haven't had a proper teenage relationship?'

'Yes,' I said.

'Well, only you can do something about that.'

I lounged around home, feeling low.

I heard about a Christian Evangelical event on the outskirts of Portsmouth. I attended one of this series of gatherings out of curiosity. The gathering was held in a huge tent, as they often are. There were gospel singers and many evangelical sermons delivered to a large crowd of people. At the end of the sermon, people were invited to come forward for the Lord if they felt something. The something, in this case, was a Christian conversion.

I knew from its reputation that Christianity was supposed to represent many good things such as charity, kindness and goodness. Much later I recognised these as collectively represented by love.

At the time I had no views on religion but was very impressed by what the Evangelist had to say. I was so impressed that I wanted to encourage people to come forward and tried this by walking forward myself. I walked to the front of the crowd, all the time encouraged by the Evangelist. Myself and other people who had come forward were taken to another part of the tent and were then asked questions by the Christian council.

The questions were rhetorical, 'What have you acknowledged?' a benign, old fellow asked me. I looked blank.

'You have acknowledged yourself as a sinner. What else have you acknowledged?' I was still silent.

'You have acknowledged the Lord Jesus Christ as your saviour.' The questions were still meaningless to me.

The following night I returned to the tent to do the same thing at the same time. I was asked if I had been reading a bible, especially some recommended scripture. I said I had not. They seemed sad and frustrated that I, a 'new born babe', as they called me, had not started 'drinking milk', by which they meant reading the bible.

All this time I had been adjusting to being seventeen and having left school. I would lay in the bath considering whether to continue visiting the Evangelist or not. I was considering college and what that would be like. It was a transition period.

Would there be bullying at college? Bullying was still a problem I had not dealt with, both in my own mind, as well as in real life. I could not make a social contrast between the behaviour and thinking of a seventeen-year-old and someone younger.

I received a letter congratulating me on what they thought was my 'conversion'. I was given the name of a church that was the nearest to me. I started to go to that very church that was recommended; it was a small church in Drayton.

The first ever service I attended, my father took me down by car. We stopped outside the building and were sitting in the car.

'I'm glad you're meeting people, Bill,' he paused, 'but if only you had an interest,' he shouted, almost hysterically. He hit the steering wheel on the word 'interest'.

By interest, my dad had meant something physical like football or a musical interest, like playing an instrument. He felt time was getting on and I needed something. I would have been excited by the prospect of an interest. Having an interest would have me being involved with people and meeting them. My father was angry and concerned that I was not doing this. I had not been able to do anything at all except what other people had wanted me to do.

There had been a drama group at Springfield that I had not got round to joining, there had also been a gymnastics club that I had considered joining but had not. My father frequently complained of what he thought was my selfishness.

There was an incident a year earlier; it had been snowing. My father had wanted me to help him push the car out of the snow outside our house. I told him I did not feel like it.

'You poor little bastard,' my father grunted, standing in the snow near the car. A few minutes later my father confessed to my mother that he had sworn at me.

'You were tired,' my father had stated sarcastically. My father was often complaining about me not offering to help with anything; not washing up, not putting crockery through the hatch of the kitchen to be washed up etc. He found my behaviour selfish. I was not aware of the effects of my action on others or in this case, it was a series of inactions.

One evening, I attended the pre-scheduling test at South Downs College, which was situated over Portsdown Hill. It was a basic English and Maths test, to ensure I was suited to take 'O' levels. I was seated in a classroom with a few other giggling teenagers. As usual, I felt alienated from them, as though I did not feel what they felt. I passed the pre-scheduling test.

When my brother and parents heard about this they told me that 'O' levels would be very challenging.

'You've got to work your arse off to get 'O' levels,' my brother said.

'You've got to go for it,' my father stated.

I put down for History, Geography and Sociology. Sociology was a subject I had never studied before, which I thought would make it more interesting.

The registration situation was chaotic, involving many students hustling and bustling up stairways to get signed up for courses. My tutor was called Olive Hoe, a curly haired, Irish woman.

The first few weeks were frightening, more frightening than I realised. As usual, I found it difficult to make friends in class or in the places where students congregated, like the refectory and the corridors. I found myself crying on frequent occasions around the college; it was due to a change of circumstances from what I was used to. The crying was spontaneous, without me considering it beforehand, or being able to stop myself. Now I was with people I did not know and in a place unfamiliar to me; I was more aware of these factors than I had been before.

I still had very little sense of how my behaviour would appear to others. I cried in a Geography lesson. The teacher was dictating too quickly for me to keep up, so I slammed my fist down hard on the table, causing laughter from the whole class. It had been an extremely hot, summer's day, the sweat was pouring down my forehead, mingling with the tears that filled my glasses.

'William!' the teacher snapped angrily, in response to the desk thumping. She spoke to me after class, telling me she did not expect tantrums from someone my age. My feelings had taken over from any consideration of social thinking; little awareness of social thinking existed anyway.

In the refectory, I tried chatting up a girl. I had sat down with my lunch next to her.

'Oh, how daintily you eat your chip,' I started.

'Creep! Fuck off!' She was trying to get rid of me in no uncertain terms.

Much later, when I was older, an 'aggressive, assertive, world view' self emerged. AAWV would have retorted with something like, 'Compared to you, I am dainty.' Instead I withdrew from the table and moved to another. While I sat, I wept. I wept again later on in the corridor.

A bloke I knew from Springfield's saw me and was concerned. I was passing him in the crowded, bustling corridor amongst many other students. He said hello, then realised I was weeping badly and swiftly pulled me into the toilets.

'What's wrong?' he demanded. I told him about the girl in the refectory making the particularly cruel remark; it did not occur to me to tell him that it was also because of being new to the college – I had found the bloke pretty obnoxious at school. He told me not to worry about a stupid girl. By stopping me and telling me she was not worth worrying about, he was showing compassion. It made me realise that people are not always how they seem. The bloke concerned had been so irritating at Springfield's that I almost had a fight with him. But this incident showed me that people are multi-faceted in their behaviour due to the multi-faceted parts of their personalities; one aspect of their actions can reveal a part of their inner personalities.

My feelings reached a climax when I ended up in one of the toilets crying and wailing out loud. A janitor, cleaning outside the cubicle I was in, heard me. I had gone into the toilets feeling like crying, entered one of the cubicles and broken down. I could not control myself, despite who might hear me. I knew the janitor was there and guessed he might intervene. He was sweeping nearby and knocked on the door to enquire. He tilted the cubicle door open and coaxed me out, then led me to a teacher who was told how he had found me. I now felt embarrassed and wanted to bottle it up. It had been the same on half the other occasions I had cried in college; it was embarrassing.

Had I considered the social implications of crying, I might have made a greater effort to control myself. Upon seeing my state with the janitor, the teacher had sent me to the college counsellor. He was a plump middle-aged man, with a pleasant, gentle demeanour who had once been a teacher. We began a number of sessions with us talking about a number of things, including my social understanding – or rather lack of it.

Earlier that term, I had gone into the reading room of the library and started reading a lot of *Time* magazines; I was still interested in current affairs, as I had always been. *Time* magazine offers comprehensive, in-depth analysis, plus astute historical comment. I loved reading them and would regularly take a carton full of magazines down from the shelf in the reading room and go through them.

The reading room had windows for walls through which the rest of the library was visible; the reading room was visible to the rest of the library, as was I. I would sit there, entranced in *Time*. One day, a middle-aged lady librarian came in and asked me why I was reading them – I could have replied because I enjoyed reading them, however what I did say in reply was that there was no particular reason, other than I wanted to.

I understood how the lady was reacting but had not been able to anticipate it. She continued, saying, 'You have been coming in regularly and reading *Time* magazine. Is there any particular reason?' She was right; I had been coming frequently into the reading room, over several months. 'Is there anything in particular you want to read about, or find out?'

I said, 'No.'

'You do realise *Time* is an American magazine?' I knew it, but did not care as I enjoyed reading it so much. After that I read *Time* magazine in the reading room less frequently.

The counsellor's office, like the reading room, was situated adjoining the library. It also had a large glass window facing out to the library. My counsellor once commented about me looking out of the window; he said I would frequently do it, including when we were talking. Looking back, I probably did it because I was distracted by the activity outside the room. I may have been taking in one thing like the counsellor talking to me, while trying to take in another – what was happening in the library. I had not learnt to think about one thing at a time. Looking away from someone when they talk can be considered just rude in many cases. The counsellor was pointing out that me being distracted and looking away was distracting for him.

Another thing I did that was socially distracting to him was when in a conversation, I would briefly give my apologies before walking out of the door. The counsellor highlighted this by suddenly saying, 'Excuse me Bill,' and walked out, closing the door behind him. A few minutes later, he re-entered and asked me, 'Now, what effect did that have on you, Bill; to have someone walk out in the middle of a meeting? How did you feel?' I admitted it was distracting. He told me it was an example of what I had done. We discussed it and I suggested that if he had walked out without saying anything at all, it would have heightened the effect. I also suggested that in future, I warn him that I may have to leave abruptly if I was needed for a lesson. This could apply to any other person in the same situation as him; by telling them at the beginning of a session, rather than halfway through, I was giving advance notice.

Other things we covered in the counselling sessions included me staring. While we were talking, the counsellor stopped me and asked what I thought I was looking at. I told him that I was looking at him. He told me the way I was looking at him made it look as though I was staring at a point at the back of his head, rather than at him, almost as though I was staring at the wall behind him.

There had been an incident in one of my history classes when some students had complained about me staring at them. They were three girls who sat in a row of seats to the right of me; I sat in the row of seats nearest the far wall of the classroom, close to the entrance. I was looking at them while the teacher was out of the room. The girls and the rest of the students were chatting amongst themselves; the girls started looking at me. Then they started complaining about something I was doing.

'Uuuugh, Bill,' they groaned, and started looking away. This went on for a few seconds then one said,

'Bill, will you stop screwing us out?' 'Screwing someone out', meant staring at them for too long.

'You can glance, but don't stare,' another one said. Another one underlined the point by giving me an exaggerated wide-eyed stare. This was a useful exercise for me that I could apply later in my social analysis. What the counsellor said to me about staring was also useful later on.

My counsellor demonstrated one expression I pulled while scratching my ankle. He was sitting opposite me when he said, 'Bill, if you don't mind, I'd like to show you something you just did.' He leaned to one side in his chair, in imitation of me and reached down to scratch his ankle; this action would have been more normal if he had not pulled the grotesque face whilst scratching. It involved him squinting his eyes until they were nearly shut – it was a revelation to me on seeing it. It was something that represented how I behaved and acted in front of others, without realising it. There were a dozen other things about me that people might notice and be more aware than I was.

I mentioned to the counsellor that I thought I seemed odd to other students, as by this time, some of them had told me that they found me odd – or worse.

I tried to chat up a girl in the same place I had tried to chat up the other one, in the refectory; she told me I was an idiot. One lad was making fun of me but I thought it was his friend who was instigating it, so I punched his friend, and then was going to punch him. He reacted scared by calling me a 'mental bastard'. I had trouble with another student too; it was all part of an overall bitchiness amongst the students.

Up until this time, the only stick I thought I was getting was imaginary. I had imagined other students wanted to make fun of me; it was part of a confused outlook I had at college. If I had been less confused at that age, or younger, I would have tried to understand what was going on by trying to understand each student individually. This was what I called the 'process method', which means examining something piece by piece, in order to understand the whole. This in turn would slow down the amount of information I was trying to take in, and by taking it in more gradually, I theoretically would understand it better.

I also picked my nose, and other people objected to this. One time, I was sitting reading in the library when a group of girls banged on the window to get my attention. They then told me I picked my nose. After a lecture, the same group of girls rubbed their fingers at me, imitating what I had done after I picked my nose. One boy I passed in a doorway circled his hand and sang 'Round and Round', at me. He had given me strange looks before and the 'Round and Round' was taken from a song at the time. It indicated to me that he thought I was somehow mad. When I was called a mental bastard by the lad whose friend I hit, I felt frustrated and angry, as well as hurt.

I had worried when I was younger about being 'mental'; it was a crass term that was also incorrectly applied. I, that is, AAWV (aggressive, assertive, world view), together with Social Cognitive, imagined myself lecturing the person who said it to me. I would ask him if he knew what was wrong with me in a calm manner. I also imagined myself asking him in the same calm manner if he was afraid of madness – this would be in the refectory, where the incident occurred. AAWV could even ask him if he had some relative such as an aunt or grandparent who was mentally ill; that would explain the fear.

When my counsellor heard about me hitting the other student, he was worried; this could be expected from a member of the college staff. He told me that it was not done to strike someone because they had annoyed me, he also mentioned that the Principal would come down on me if these incidents persisted.

I had wanted to prove myself 'hard', to stop people picking on me and insulting me. At seventeen years-old, I was doing it at a late stage. When I had had the confrontation with Mark Burns, he had run away, and my father had commented then, 'If only you had done that from the outset and established your reputation as a hard boy.' I knew this but had not carried it out – that is until I was attacked by Mark Burns.

At seventeen I had been in hardly any fights at all. I mentioned this to my tutor and about me wanting to be hard. She told me there were other ways I could be hard, such as with a few 'well spoken words'. By this she meant being assertive and lecturing people rather than hitting them; AAWV would later help me realise this.

When my counsellor heard about me wanting to be hard he said it was not how he would want to be. At this time, physical aggression was the only way I could think of as an effective form of communication. The counsellor also agreed with my tutor that there were other ways I could stand up for myself, without being physically hard. He pointed to ways I could turn social situations around with clever remarks; he had noted in his conversations with me that I had a sense of humour. He said my sense of humour might be used to throw a clever remark back at someone in the course of a conversation; to date, I was more likely to be on the receiving end of amusing or clever remarks, than handing them out.

AAWV would have thought of things I could have said in certain situations, such as when the lad I punched came out with, 'My friend says you wash your private parts in wash basins.' I could have replied,'Only if you'd fondle them!'

Again, when the lad I punched said, 'Know what a corkscrew is? You're as bent as one.' I might have quipped,

'At least I'd have better taste in men.'

The counsellor also talked about the manner in which I said things, in relation to both being aggressive and assertive. He had been a teacher and demonstrated how he had said things in an angry manner during his former career; he raised his voice, making it sharper. I was not all that familiar with the manner in which something was said, as opposed to what was being said. I was still scared of being suddenly shouted at, so had not thought about raising my voice. I had not yet learnt to harness and express my emotions, any emotions that is, that were developing.

Chapter 8

Friends

*N*ot all my experience with other students and young people were bad. I was sitting at a desk when a bloke came up to me and started talking. His name was Stephen Ferguson. I had seen him in my history class and he had said hello occasionally. He was tall and about my age. Up until this time, I had judged him as a bit rough, due to his accent and dress; it was this, together with his height that made him seem intimidating. On this particular occasion he was very affable; he told me about his approach to people he met, and about being part of a social grouping. He said he would start by making a bit of a fool of himself when he was with other people – he must have done this to break the ice. He told me he believed that life should be full of laughs, and that he hung around the college with groups of people, especially in the refectory and the empty classrooms. He went on to talk about the course he was doing; in addition to History he was also studying English and when he left college he planned to join the Navy and then the police force. He invited me to spend time with other young people in the refectory and elsewhere, the way he did.

Being invited to spend time with other people my age was a revelation to me – and a relief. I had been constantly trying to get into a social grouping, or form a social relationship with someone my own age. A year earlier I had been lonely, now I was experiencing my first proper friendship in seventeen years. I had been provided with a sense of trust that helped me to connect with another person; it helped to make up for seventeen years' inability to experience what most other people had; lack of experience had become self-perpetuating. I had not spent time with groups of people at school or elsewhere. I had not known how to break in socially. It was as though the people in the group all knew something I did not or had learnt something I had not.

I invited Stephen to our house; my mother was delighted that I had a friend. She made us beans on toast to eat and sat down to talk to Steve. Later, Steve and I sat together in my bedroom; I wandered in and out. The things Steve and I talked about were quite mundane, such as the posters of pretty girls I had on my wall, and current affairs.

I found taking to one person about simple things was a lot easier than talking to a large group about more things. In large groups, students tended to talk more quickly, answering each other and finishing each other's sentences off. It was more confusing for me. Having Steve around, I felt I was doing what I would have liked to have done about eight years earlier.

I was still awkward with other students and one of my odd habits was still running round the college. Once, I crossed a girl's path as she was walking up the stairs. She called me a 'Wally'. What I did not realise at the time was that running round a crowded college was not just odd, it was also dangerous since I might collide with someone. I did not automatically realise this practical, logical fact.

When it came to relations with others, my counsellor advised me to listen, as well as talk. I had established more social contact with Steve and his friends, and outside college there was the Church. There were many young people I saw in church services but I had not struck up a relationship with any of them as yet.

There was a musical session involving keyboards and a choir as part of the church service, after which I invited one of the blokes back to my house for a drink. Everyone else had left and he was just packing his keyboard away. I decided I would make the effort to establish a relationship with someone, so I started chatting with him then asked him back for a drink, he agreed.

My parents were impressed by Ross Reserve as he sat in our living room and talked about himself. After a few more meetings, involving activities organised by the church such as walks, Ross revealed that he had also studied at South Downs College. He also revealed that he had found it difficult not to feel left out socially too. One of the things he advised was not to daydream, 'Because if you daydream you end up looking like this.' He impersonated a vacant expression with a slightly open mouth. 'And if you look like that, you'll look weird and there is no way a girl is going to go out with someone who appears a like a weirdo.'

I asked him what he would daydream about in college; he said it was about himself as the head of a family. The daydream he experienced was far more realistic than any of mine had ever been. Mine had always been related to films and television and what was not reality; at the time it did not occur to me to tell him that. On the subject of relationships with others, especially students, he said it was best to be casual and allow relationships to happen. This reminded me of something Maurice had once told me when I was at school; he told me a simple greeting or acknowledgement could be the first step in a relationship and did not have to be forced.

Ross told me what I needed was something I could do that I was good at, like an interest.

'An interest,' he told me, 'might help you to make friends because it would be something you would have in common with them.' He also said it might help me feel better in myself. Ross's interest was music and to my knowledge he played in a rock band.

On the subject of people and understanding them, Ross recalled a book by Dale Carnegie called, *How to Win Friends and Influence People*. I later bought the book from a bookshop and started reading it. Ross, when he heard I was reading it, said that some of the later chapters dealt with how to get people to do things for you, this was in relation to organising people in an office or some other workplace. The chapter as I remember, dealt with remembering people's names; it also dealt with smiling at people. The counsellor had talked to me about smiling; he said it might make a difference in the way people responded to me. Once, while I was talking to him, he looked at me in a very dull and gloomy way. It was a face that looked still and lifeless, the way I must have looked then – it was an imitation of me. He did it to show what I looked like when I didn't smile. Smiling was something I did do, the only problem was it was smiling to myself, and that made me look odd. I would smile continuously; it was when I imagined things that amused me. These were jokes I had heard or things I had seen on television, or things that I had thought of myself. Sometimes it could manifest itself in a slight smile, other times it could be a big broad grin. There was one occasion, back at Springfield's school when a teacher complained about me grinning in class. The grin had been broad enough and constant enough for Mr Bentley, the humanities teacher, to notice. A similar incident had happened before then at Manor

Court. Both teachers had told me to stop it.

I found time spent with Steve and his friends was awkward but bearable – I was doing something that I had little experience of. At Springfield there had been some pupils I spent time with and when I talked to them I tended to talk about what I wanted to talk about, things like horror films that had been on television.

There was one particular time I was with a group of Steve's friends in a classroom during either a free period or lunchtime. There had been a programme on TV a few days earlier; it was a made-for-TV film that dealt with a mentally handicapped man called Walter. The film had the same title. Steve's group of friends were casually discussing it and one or two asked if that was me in the film playing Walter. At the time, I realised they were kidding me, as young men do, so I was not hurt; they were friends of my friend Steve, so I knew I could trust them socially. Also, I may have subconsciously realised that they thought I had something wrong with me mentally. That was one social approach to the situation. Anther social approach to the situation was the broad one. To imagine they were making the sort of joke they could have made to anyone, regardless of their circumstances. I myself had seen the film *Walter* and realised the character's mental handicap was very mild, compared to my own.

I met a girl at the college who openly stated to me that she was retarded. She was very pretty and very nervous in her manner, but whilst I still had no confidence either, I was convinced that unlike her, I was not retarded. The boyfriend of the retarded girl seemed very protective of her. He also showed a certain jealousy when I talked to her and when I seemed closer to her socially. Did he sense I was somehow mentally handicapped myself, which gave me an advantage by having a sense of empathy with her?

Later on I could have reasoned away any thoughts of being retarded by understanding what the term meant. Maurice Bridgeland and a few others had frequently told me that I was intelligent and I was later to discover that I was above average intelligence; it was a few years after I studied GCSEs at college when my parents took me to see a psychiatrist and we discussed what was wrong with me. The psychiatrist ruled our retardation, as retarded people did not get GCSEs; what he said helped me to gain a precise, fixed idea of mental retardation. This in turn contrasted with concepts of other mental handicaps and mental illnesses.

Some of Steve's friends, had compared me with Walter, the mentally handicapped individual, played by Ian McKellen. It was ironic if they thought I was mentally handicapped myself. The Walter on television was obviously retarded; I was doing GCSEs. It may also have been ironic of me to think that they had made the remark because they thought I was mentally handicapped. My learning disability was a lack of evaluation of what others said in relation to certain things; I could also fail to note the complexity of them.

I had little trouble with other students, apart from the few skirmishes with the bloke who called me a mental bastard and his friend that I punched. I had once asked my father why people picked on me and he said it was because I was not 'one of the herd'; I did not fit into the culture of people my age.

One way I did not fit into to the culture was by not being as sociable as many of them were. My father had advised me to try to sympathise with people my own age. When I asked him what he meant by sympathise, he said to think how they think. Later on, I was able to understand this in terms of empathy, but that was later in my life.

Chapter 9

Trouble with the Tech Block

*T*he only other trouble I was getting was from a group in college who were doing what I was told were 'technical courses'. They were frightening to me because of the way they looked and talked. A few of them had come to me in the library and informed me there was a rumour going round that I was a homosexual; they used the term, 'Crispi', after the famous homosexual, Quentin Crisp. They teased me all they liked because they thought I was unaggressive, but that idea was partly challenged when I got hold of my main teaser in the corridor and demanded, 'What course are you doing?' I was going to tell him to get on with it, rather than bothering with me. He told me it was none of my business. I was holding his jacket as I punched him on the cheek; his glasses went flying, landing near the top of the stairs.

We wrestled for a few minutes then broke off. He demanded that I pick up his glasses. I just stood silently, so he picked them up himself but went on to demand that I apologise. I said nothing and walked off.

Later, Maurice Bridgeland said I was justified in getting angry and hitting him. The question I had asked, 'What course are you doing?' was perfectly normal and reasonable he said.

Maurice told me that people picked on me because I was supposed to be weak but the fact of the matter was that the people who did it, he said, were often weak themselves. We were having a session as we drove home in his car. I told him there was a rumour going round that I was gay – according to a few people at college. Maurice seemed a bit sad about this. He suggested it might have started because I had not shown any real interest in girls, not enough interest for anyone to notice. Maurice said that when he picked me up near the gate, he had noticed a quite attractive girl that I could perhaps approach. The only girls I had had contact with in the past seemed uncouth and had teased me; this had been at school and briefly at college. There had been nice girls who said hello to me, just as there had been blokes who had been friendly but these people, however, just passed me by.

I had tried chatting up a few girls at the college, to little or no avail. One girl, small blonde and pretty, had mentioned she was engaged only a few minutes after I tried to strike up a conversation with her; it seemed to me that she might have been deliberately trying to distance herself from me.

The theory about why I was rumoured to be gay was not just about showing no interest in girls, it was about showing little interest in people generally. A person who is a loner can easily be perceived as odd amongst young people, where social interaction tends to be very active, and where the odd person can be perceived as alienated from the entire social group. Since the social group falls into two parts, male and female, the 'alien' may be perceived as not fitting into one group or the other, thus bringing into question the 'alien's' sexuality. This can happen subconsciously in the minds of the social group.

My father was baffled and hurt that I was still being bullied. I, on the other hand, had almost come to accept it; it had happened all the way through my school and college life, which is what hurt my father. What I had come to accept were my own imagined incidents of bullying and the imagined frequency that they took place. My brother had always been more casual about it; he just kept urging me to have friends.

One particular time, I had been ascending some stairs when some rather 'oikish' looking students passed me; they might have been from the technical block. Just after passing me, one of them made a gesture – he covered his backside with his hands; this was an obvious indication he thought I was gay. His mates giggled about it.

I had a feeling on seeing this, which I mentioned to my counsellor. My counsellor asked me what I thought the feeling was. 'Anger,' I replied. My counsellor said that by thinking of it as anger, I was recognising it as anger. If that was how I was feeling on the stairs, then I could have recognised the feeling as being angry and expressed it. Expressing anger to the lads on the stairs may have only led to more trouble with the technical block students. Also, if it was to do with a rumour I could not refute then it may have only made the rumour worse.

The only emotion I had been experiencing up until then had been fear. Fear may have been partly responsible for a lot of the tantrums and anger I experienced. These were crude basic emotions that I did not fully recognise and did not think about. My emotional self had not been broken down into lots of different emotions. Just as my thinking should have been determined by what the situation was, i.e. social cognition, so my emotions should have been determined according to the context. My thinking and emotions should have been acting in unison; in most cases the emotional self should have followed on from the cerebral self.

I felt only extreme emotions such as fear and anger, which both stemmed from lack of rational thought. Rational thought would have tempered these extreme emotions. I felt emotions such as the ones that had me blubbering in the toilets but was not aware of them.

My counsellor mentioned that I called the other students 'kids', when I referred to my peers.

'But the way you're talking about it, Bill,' my counsellor started, 'you're referring to them as kids in a way that makes them sound like children.' He paused, looking at me. 'You talk about yourself being a kid. Does this mean you consider yourself to be a child?'

'It must have been the way I used the term kids,' I said, in a flat, matter-of-fact way that lacked any lively, relaxed element. I had picked up the term, 'the kids' from newspapers and television, knew that it meant young people and thought it seemed a normal term to use. But, I did not realise that the manner in which a term is used can be just as important as the term itself. If I had known this fact, I had not been able to apply or exercise it.

The emotional self affects the manner in which a person says something. This is the broad range of emotions they feel that affects their tone of voice. I had no real emotional range and so, I had nothing to affect my voice or knowledge to inflect it. My father had once said that he found my voice difficult to understand and hear because it was not inflected; its pitch did not vary, becoming higher or lower.

My previous counsellor once videotaped me and him in one of our sessions then played it back to me in the next one. I told him that I was shocked by what I had seen and heard of myself. I found my speech and movements very stilted as I sat down on the chair talking to the counsellor; my voice was very slow and sounded dull. It seemed to come out in grunts, as and when it was totally audible – even my own ears had trouble hearing it!

When I told the college counsellor all this he responded by saying, 'You don't like yourself very much, do you Bill?'

'My previous counsellor made the video to show me how I looked and acted,' I replied. Later, AAWV would have said that it was helpful in providing me with a model that I could improve. It was an example of how I behaved, which could be modified and improved in terms of how my voice sounded, what my gestures were and how my posture appeared.

In one of our early sessions, my college counsellor told me my movements were very exaggerated; this was probably due to my body being very tense. There was a time in Springfield in the youth club when a particularly nasty boy had been imitating me picking up rubbish. He had imitated the way I walked; it was a timid walk that tiptoed while talking long strides – it almost seemed the boy was doing me a favour by showing me how I walked. It seemed the sort of walk done by someone who thought too much about simple tasks, and was thus very tense. It indicated a lack of any continual concentration, as well as an inability to do things naturally and spontaneously. Thinking too much was a form of over-introspection. My autism had made me introverted and a loner, and being a loner made me more introverted – it was all part of a big circle.

The counsellor had asked me about friends and why we have them and whilst we were discussing it he asked me if I could think of the advantages of having friends. He repeated the question at the end of the session and set it as an exercise for me to do until the next meeting.

I was still lonely; I would get frustrated and sad, despite now having Steve as a friend my own age. Once, I was on a bus home from a disco in Southsea, I felt my mind wailing for friends my own age. I was trying to penetrate how other teenagers thought, acted and behaved. Ross Reserve had told me he ended up playing cards in one of the classrooms at lunchtime. This was something I never did at college; I spent all my time reading in the library. I had been with groups of people but had not properly broken into groups.

At college, I was walking up some stairs in the same part of the building I had encountered the 'oikish' students. I passed another group of 'oikish' students at the stairway's top.

'Oh, here comes Crispi,' a tall, heavily built student said, Crispi meaning me. Later I passed the same group at the same spot near the stairs; the bloke I had argued with, whose glasses I had knocked off was with them. He moved to nudge against me, presumably because I had punched him. I put out my hand to push him away and resist his intimidation, but because I was walking past him, my hand started pushing, then ended up just brushing against him. The rest of the group laughed; I had not thought quickly enough, I should have pulled my hand down as I was getting further from him.

I wander now if Asperger's Syndrome has any effect on a subject's physical movement or mental condition. I read somewhere that the condition affects some subjects' stance; certainly a person's physical movements can affect what others think when they see them. It is similar to how a person's verbal statements affect what others think when they hear them. Maurice Bridgeland once said that the problem of not knowing how other people work might be physically related. Maurice also mentioned that when a person eye-witnessed social behaviour, such as how a person walked and moved, it may not send the right messages to the brain. The same thing might apply to the ear when it heard what a person said and how they said it.

The big lad who called me Crispi intimidated me; he had

intimidated me because he was big. It may have been partly subconscious fear, but I was afraid of his size; deep down I was afraid of everyone. I was still out to try and prove myself, as well as try to deal with the rumour that I was gay, (or as the big student had said, 'Crispi'). I saw the big student walking towards me in the corridor; he was flanked by two others from his group. One of them, the smaller one, said something to me as I drew closer; it contained the word, 'Crispi'. It was the big, heavily built student I was interested in.

'Did you call me 'Crispi'?' I asked him.

'Yes,' he replied. I drew back my fist as he came closer and tried to hit him. I missed. He pushed me against the lockers and told me he wasn't hitting me because I wore glasses. I did not know what was going to happen next, but then fortunately a teacher shouted and broke us up. He ushered the big student into another room and took his name down; the big student continued to protest, saying that he would 'ave me', while giving me a look. When I met the same teacher again, he told me to smile at the big student and say, 'You silly bugger,' in an inoffensive way.

When I repeated this to Maurice Bridgeland, he expressed the fear that the way I said, 'You silly bugger,' might be construed as a literal attack. This might lead to the student taking offence and reacting violently. Maurice also expressed concern that I might attack someone bigger than me. I might end up saying, 'You silly bugger' in a serious way because I found it difficult to express myself in a relaxed way; everything I said tended to be expressed in a serious, worried way.

The studying itself was proving hard; I did most of it at home; history was the hardest. I would frequently get angry and shout when I could not remember it; I would go to my room to study and forty-five minutes later my parents would hear me wailing. This was because I tried getting a large amount of reading into my head and couldn't do it. I tried getting my parents to test me. One time, my father asked me a question from the notes in the folder; I hesitated, or gave half an answer and my father sat in the armchair in the dining room, getting frustrated, then he let out a low scream-cum-shout. He swiftly closed the folder, threw it down on a nearby stool, picked up a newspaper and swiftly started reading it. I had not yet mastered the technique of learning through thinking, which is learning facts through trying to understand them, rather than just trying to remember them.

There was to be more trouble with the technical block students, instigated by the big student.

At a college disco I met an old school friend and mentioned to him that I was getting stick from the kids in the technical block.

'Ignore them,' he had told me with a gentle smile as we sat at a table. 'Ignore them, Bill. They're not doing the same course as you.'

I passed one of the technical block students at the same place I had passed them before, at the top of the stairs and he made a remark to me about me hitting the big student, which was untrue, 'Because he called you 'Crispi', which you are.'

'No, I'm not,' I retorted.

'Yes, you are,' he said.

'No. I'm not,' I repeated.

'Yes, you are,' he said. 'You want to fight me?'

I walked away from the stairs then found myself walking back up the stairs again. I realised I had never been in a proper fight.

'Alright then,' I said when I got to him. We both went downstairs and out of the college. I wanted to fight him to see what it was like. I did not get hurt but I did not come off best; I lost the fight.

I had hit a few blokes before but had not been able to mentally reconcile the act of striking someone; it was something I had not been able to do at the right time and place.

The next day, I met Olive Hoe, my tutor, and she mentioned that she had heard of the trouble I had the previous day. I told her it was because I wanted to prove myself hard and that I was also curious about experiencing physical violence. Olive told me there were other ways I could act hard, such as with words; AAWV would later prove more adept at this. Olive told me the effect of what happened only made me look stupid to the technical block students, and others; it was the humiliating effect of losing a fight. She had a serious discussion with me about it there in the corridor, reminding me I could get seriously hurt, which was something I had not considered. She also told me that as I wore glasses they might get broken and glass could stick in my eye. I told her I could take them off, like I did in the first fight.

I had worn glasses since I was fifteen but had not yet understood the social, and in this case physical, implications of wearing them. My father had told me his theory that people who wore glasses tended to be more introverted than people who did not but I had been introverted through most of my childhood. I had also been partially short sighted; I needed glasses to see the blackboard at school and to watch television. My father kept telling me I had to wear my glasses more at school so I could see the people who teased me and thus avoid them. I had a few remarks from people after I started wearing them full time.

'What an intelligent looking young man,' a boy had once said in Woolworths department store, situated at the top of

Cosham High Street. I had passed him as I strolled in, his girlfriend, who was working behind a counter, motioned for him to be quiet upon hearing his remark. The remark he made had been a subtle attack rather than a direct one, but at that age it passed me by, as I did not appreciate it properly.

At college, the counsellor reacted to the fight the same way he reacted to the other tensions. He told me violence was not the way forward, whether for moral reasons or under the rules of the college. He also warned me of potential disciplinary action that might be taken if I persisted fighting; fighting, he warned was something the college felt very strongly about. He said I should take being called 'Crispi' with a pinch of salt, since boys or young men called each other 'poof' and homosexual as a form of horseplay. By rights, the way the students behaved was not horseplay, since the insults were not playful and they were not exchanged between friends. I had not fully realised this.

Whenever the big, tall lad saw me, he would shout out, 'Crispi'. I tried to avoid him by avoiding the places where I knew he would be, such as the outside common room.

'Alright Din,' he once said as I passed him.

'My name's Bill,' I said defiantly.

'Bill Din,' he quipped.

Later I thought of things AAWV could have said to him, such as, 'That's a big word for you to use,' in reply to being called Din or 'You study at the technical block don't you? Bet you couldn't spell it!' These retorts would have been made mainly for amusement but on reflection, I realise they may have led to further trouble. What AAWV could have said was, 'Look, I didn't come here to fight and argue with people, I came here to study, so you keep to your course and I'll keep to mine, right?' It might have had an effect but it would be more about the way I said it than what I said, and I couldn't be sure that I could say it with the right conciliatory inflection. Equally, I could have tried looking at the lad in the eye without staring through him, as I did with other people.

The first time I saw the big student again after trying to hit him, he gave me an exaggerated beady look and then called me, 'a real Dinlow'. I could have said that I was doing GCSEs so I did not qualify as a Dinlow; I could have said that in response to being called a Din as well. A Dinlow or Din is a Portsmouth term for fool or idiot.

My run-ins with the big lad and his friends from the technical block came to a head one day when I was in the library, either reading or studying. I was in full view of the corridor through the library's window; I was trying to evade the big student but paradoxically wanted to confront him and try to resolve the situation, which was why I sat in full view of the corridor!

Eventually, I heard a loud tapping and looked up to see my tormentor giving me the finger. He went away and a few minutes later reappeared with the lad I lost the fight to. They bustled through the library doors, talking loudly about attacking someone without warning or without reason being totally out of order. I was scared because the big student was big, over six foot tall and fifteen stone in weight. It was only after I had attacked him that I realised how big he was – even Stephen Ferguson, my six-foot best friend had expressed concern about how big he was.

They came over and sat opposite me. I started to apologise for attacking the big student, whilst they started telling me about how the rumour of me being homosexual had begun. Another student from the technical block came in and sat down. The first two started trying to cause trouble between me and him. I should have avoided them; they were trying to needle me but I could not read the situation.

'What are you thinking about?' the smaller one asked me in the middle of me talking; he probably said that because I was not focused at the time. I had been looking through him or generally looking odd. We went outside into the corridor where they continued telling me I had to do something about the rumour or they would continue. Finally, I told them I was ignoring them from now on as they were just trying to annoy me.

'Cripsi,' the big one called out as I went back into the library.War had resumed. The counsellor agreed that they were just trying to needle me rather than make contact with me, as I had suggested.

When I had asked the big student his name out of curiosity, he had replied, 'Fred Blogs', mocking me, then he paused and said, 'Dave Potter'.

I tried making contact with other people when I used the library, but sadly it seems that the people I took most notice of were the people who attacked me; I took more notice of them because they attacked me. I had wanted to get to know them because they scared me, not just because they were bigger than me but because they looked, behaved and talked in a threatening manner. It was the same as it had been at school, the people in question, like Mark Burns, were more threatening than most. If I had been more able to judge social situations, I would not have attacked the big student as it was unreasonable, but if I had attacked him in retaliation for attacking me, it would have been more understandable. My counsellor, Maurice Bridgeland and other teachers were right – attacking someone for no reason was out of order; another fact related to whether it was justified or not was timing, and the time when it might have been justified had now passed. That was the social and behavioural aspect of attacking someone; the other was legal.

Under law it does not matter how much bigger or 'harder' the person you attack is, or whether he has an advantage, such as having others with him, it is the act itself that gets dealt with by the courts. The big student, or the big anyone who is attacked would have been legally entitled to take me to court, or even in this case to the police. Being attached by someone you don't know can be a criminal case.

I did not know these things at the time, or that the social and legal aspects were related. I, together with the big student and his smaller mate, were one year away from legally becoming adults – that is if we were not legally adults already, being over sixteen.

At the time I was coming up to eighteen and I could not believe it. Adulthood had rushed upon me; I could not believe it. Adulthood had rushed upon me and over me, without me realising it. I remembered when I had talked to my counsellor about calling other students 'kids'; he had told me I was calling them children and by example, calling myself a child. I was a child no longer.

Because I understood only crude, basic emotions, I became worried that feeling angry would distract me from my studies. The next time I met Maurice, he told me it was a pity I did not enjoy college as a learning experience; not just going there, but actually to enjoy it, making new friends and more social contact. I had made some social progress with Steve Ferguson so the whole thing had not been wasted. The experiences I had had, good or bad, were better than no experiences at all.

'Why do they pick on me?' I had asked, again. It was a question I asked out of curiosity rather than any sense of self-pity. I knew part of the answer.

'Because you don't hit back.' This was something I had tried to make up for by hitting out and trying to be hard. I had attempted this from the beginning with few real results, as it was too late. There had been frequent sarcastic remarks about my mild reputation, 'Oh, please Bill, don't hit me,' a student from the technical block once said, as he pretended to cower. He was one of the people I did eventually hit.

'I heard you did five blokes,' another student had ironically stated, without malice.

'Alright Ultra,' another had said, sneering as I walked past.

Another reason they picked on me was because I was different. This I knew; I knew that I was embarrassing being different and it caused me to be picked on, but I could do very little about it.

Not all of what had happened at college was bad. The big student had been looking at job applications once when I encountered him – he was in the corridor with his mates.

'Got a job yet Crisps?' he asked, as I drew near. When Maurice heard this he began to tell me about 'social turn ons' and 'social turn offs'.

'When you pass someone you know without saying hello to them, then it's a social turn off, however when you pass someone you know and say hello to them, then it's a social turn on.' These were things I knew already; I could understand them but could not properly apply them. I needed to be told things repeatedly until I was able to apply it by myself. I could apply things better by learning rather than just remembering.

I had told Maurice I wanted to think of the bullies as so low as to view them as not worth thinking about, in order not to get angry. Maurice replied by saying this attitude would cover half the rough, anti-social types he saw. Maurice saw these people as part of his child psychology career, which included people that threatened others on the street.

On the subject of anger interrupting my studies, Maurice got me to lie back on the bed which I was sitting on in his office and relax – I could then tell him all that happened between me and the two students. He told me to put all my thinking about the students aside and simply forget it; this was sooner said than done. I had not yet learnt how to control bad thoughts.

One good incident had occurred at college in General Studies. I had revealed that I did not have any friends or social contact. The students had first reacted impatiently, telling me only I could change things, but afterwards, a girl told me I might make friends if I went out to pubs. I did this later on, mainly to Uncle Tom's Cabin, at the top of Cosham where I met a large group of blokes whom I almost went to a nightclub with. I also met blokes from the college there.

Another good person I met at the college was a lecturer called Nina Cooper, my sociology teacher. She was half black and had an easy charm, despite a tendency to get angry very quickly. I had some very interesting talks with her after class; she was well informed and could relax the student-teacher barrier. We talked about the social and philosophical aspects of life but rarely about the socially cognitive.

The socially cognitive aspect means the way people relate to each other; relationships between people. I once asked Nina if she had studied psychology to which she said, yes. I then asked her if she knew what a 'personality defect' was. She seemed to get annoyed, rounding on me and saying, 'Bill, go and talk to other sociology students.' She felt I was getting too wrapped up in myself, too introspective and less concerned about others. It seemed selfish to her; I knew what she meant when she got annoyed, but it had not stopped me asking in the first place. I had only asked because I knew there may be something wrong with me but did not know what. Maurice had told me my problem of not understanding people was part of what was called a 'personality defect'. The term possibly applies to how a person behaves as a symptom of a kind of defect.

Walking up to South Downs at the beginning of the year, I had met a bloke I had gone to Springfield with who had told me that I used to run around at school. On hearing this I was embarrassed, I even apologised to the bloke, in a manner of sorts. If running around at school had been combined with laughing to myself, it added to the embarrassment. He told me not to worry about it.

At the time I was more aware of what I had been doing at school than what I was doing at college, and was concerned. I was trying to make up for the time I had lost. I wanted to change my behaviour by being more aware of it. Certain things like my bad experience with the technical block students and Mark Burns had made me more aware of myself and the social situation I was in. I was determined not to let the scars of my experience with the two students affect me, or my future, the same way my experience with Mark Burns had.

Chapter 10

Employment Rehabilitation Centre

*I*was now back on the job market *and,* through a lot of frustrating, hard work I now had two 'O' levels – as they were known then – in English and History; Sociology had fallen through. When not looking for work, I was spending money on things like sweets, crisps and occasionally cream cakes. I may have spent money on those things due to boredom. I had done this before and would continue to do so.

I was getting twenty-five pounds a week in dole money; as I was later to discover, this was less than I would have earned in a job. At the time, it was more than I had ever received and I spent it on things that gratified me. When not doing this, I was using the job centre and the *Evening News* to look for work. I had been doing this before I went to college.

Because I had never worked, I was given a place on a course at an Employment Rehabilitation Centre. The purpose of the course was to find out what a person was good at to recommend them to an employer; it lasted for six weeks. I was together with twelve to thirteen other men, and a few women at the beginning.

The Employment Rehabilitation Centre was a stark collection of buildings resembling a small factory. It was located in Hilsea and its factory look was heightened by the workbenches that were in the buildings and the workbenches that dotted the centre. The course was held in a main classroom.

When the centre's large, grey-haired manager finished one of the first lectures, he asked us what we thought the average weekly wage would be for the average worker. I said the lowest possible wage – to encourage an employer to employ us and so that we were not too expensive to employ. The manager said, if we proposed that in an interview, the employer would think we were less keen on the job since we did not want much for it and suggested saying we could begin on ninety pounds a week, then go on to one hundred and thirty.

If someone had asked me then and there what I thought the average weekly wage was, I would not have been able to say; this was because I did not know. If I had been asked about something I had covered in 'O' level History, such as Stalin, Hitler or Prohibition, I may have been able to answer. Later, when I met some old friends from Springfield in the Uncle Tom's Cabin pub in Cosham, I discovered they had jobs. The jobs earned them around one hundred to one hundred and twenty pounds per week.

How much someone earned in a job depended of course on how much they would need for food, rent, clothes, gas and what was necessary for everyday survival. It was only later that I would learn about day-to-day survival.

My brother once said that all I knew about life was from television, which was not relevant to everyday life and was rubbish. If I had spent time with people my own age when I was younger, I would have learnt more about many things. For example a boy telling me how much his father earned in his job would have helped me understand how much an average worker earned. The money issue was really one of balance, depending on realistic needs. An employee should not demand too much that is more than he needs. Neither should he demand too little, which is less than he needs.

The course began with me being put on painting. I was set to painting some pieces of wood, to find out how good I was at it. I painted one or two the way I had been shown then stopped; it did not occur to me to carry on painting more. I lacked the initiative for a work situation; this was something that I felt more as time went on. I waited for the supervisor to come and tell me to do another piece of wood.

When I told Maurice what I was doing he said it would be good for me to learn carpentry and painting, especially for when I had my own place. I arranged an interview with the manager of the course saying I would like to learn more about practical things like painting and DIY. I did not actually say DIY but said it was for the reasons Maurice suggested.

The manager looked at the door and asked, 'How would you paint that door?' He was really referring to the fact that the course was to enhance and improve skills people already had; I had no experience of any practical skill or trade.

Practical cognitive would have said, 'Paint the wood in a certain way with certain strokes so it does not drip. Paint it again to form another layer. Paint two or three layers then varnish it. I might also have to do something to the door before actually beginning to paint.' These were the ideas practical cognitive would have had – if it had existed at the time. Despite being very impractical, both then and now, it would have helped to have practical cognitive, it would have been better than nothing.

I told the manager that using skills for DIY had been the idea of someone I knew. He was looking at me with a hard gaze, and did not say anything. I admitted, 'It was just a silly idea.'

'Well, we don't go in for silly ideas here. We go in for careful, reasoned thinking. Forget what this other person told you, this shows you weren't listening to what I said at the beginning;' he paused, 'which isn't a very good opener. Is it?'

What practical cognitive would have said was, 'I was listening to what you said at the beginning, it's just that I said something different from what you said, rather than repeating what you said word for word.' I might also have told the manager that I was saying this because I was thinking about what the situation was, as opposed to not thinking.

'From this,' he continued, 'and from reports I'm getting, I'm becoming very worried.' I did not know what he meant. 'Unless I see some changes, things aren't going to improve.' I left puzzled by all the things he had said.

Practical cognitive would have asked him what he was getting at. He had assumed I had not been listening, but I could have indicated that I was listening to what was said but had not understood. However, if I had said that, people might think I was just thick. This is one of the things social cognitive would have realised.

I went back to the tasks set for me at the centre. These included office work that I had expressed a preference for and gardening. Office work included filing, copying things out, whilst gardening included digging out weeds from the edge of the centre.

The memory of South Downs College and the trouble with the students was clawing at me. This was despite my hopes that it wouldn't; I felt angry. Maurice had told me the anger was not just towards people who mistreated me but was about the other things as well; one of these could have been an inability to socially extend myself. The memories of college became too much to bear so I made an appointment with the social worker; I was hoping she could help me with personal stuff too.

She was sitting at her desk in her office as I went in and showed little interest in me; she was looking down at something she was writing. I told her about my feelings and how they had become a problem for me. Then I went on to tell her how I had been treated at South Downs and how I felt right to be angry about it.

'And what did you do?' she asked, meaning what did I do about the way I was treated.

'Nothing,' I replied. 'That's the problem, sometimes my anger leads to depression.' It sounded like something a psychologist would say; the social worker herself said it sounded like something out of psychologist's handbook. If I had known or realised it sounded like this I would have expressed it in a different way. I did sense it sounded strange as I was saying it but did not definitely know it in my mind.

When I asked her what I could do to help my feelings, she suggested talking it out. 'Oh! I felt I could punch him in the face,' she said mimicking the kind of thing said in pubs and elsewhere. This was to get it off my chest. Then she went on to say, 'If I'm doing a job,' she meant one of the jobs at the centre or elsewhere, 'I can't afford to be thinking about my concentration affecting the job. What will you do if you meet this person?' She meant the smaller of the two students.

'Break his nose,' I replied. My feelings prevented me from holding back verbally and saying something I regretted. At that time I had no idea if I should hold back from saying anything embarrassing.

She asked me if breaking his nose would make me feel better.

'Yes,' I said.

'Very well then,' she said darkly. 'If you get pleasure from breaking people's noses, then that's your problem!'

She could not empathise with my problems and did not understand them; what she said about me breaking the student's nose did make me think. There had been a bloke sitting next to her who mentioned assault charges upon hearing that I wanted to attack my one-time tormentor. At South Downs the student had taken the valves out of my tyres, which had admittedly made me very angry, but there would still have been consequences if I had actually attacked him.

This was the moral effect of what I said. I had stated I wanted to inflict damage on another human being, which might shock the people who heard it. If I had known this I would not have said it. Likewise the situation might have been affected by the manner I had expressed myself: 'like a psychologist's handbook'. If I was socially and emotionally balanced I would have thought in a different way and would not have felt emotional enough to make the statement in the first place; I would have had more control.

Aggressive Assertive World View (AAWV) later produced a 'personal view', through which I could have told the social worker that some people are confident enough not to be afraid of certain types of people; they didn't hate them, they just didn't have anything to prove. AAWV and social cognitive would have both said these things through me. I would have said that being wise and confident would have helped me not to be afraid, and thus aggressive. I would have mentioned to the social worker the personal and moral effects of what I had said – this was part of social cognition, the process of understanding the effect of what a person says has on others. I would have stated that I may not have needed to physically hurt a person nor claim that I would enjoy it. I would have also said that by controlling and channelling my anger I could come to terms with it, and that it could be expressed in more acceptable ways such as through assertiveness, which would then be part of AAWV.

I had no particular views or feelings; whatever views or feelings I had were not focussed ones. I had not yet come to gauge other people and thus had no views or feelings about them. The views and feelings concerning the blokes at college were based on crude unfocused emotions, which did not amount to proper estimations.

I left the interview without feeling any better. If Aggressive Assertive World View had been there it would have told her that lack of confidence was part of the reason for my treatment at college, and was also part of the reason I could not forgive and forget the two students. Lack of confidence equalled fear, and fear equalled anger. AAWV would make me more confident by being more assertive.

I tried talking to a few people at the Employment Rehabilitation Centre. There was a young man who would talk to me spontaneously for long periods. I hardly needed to strike up a conversation, he would talk to me anyway. He was far more sociable than me, which made him different in his manner of speech and movement – he may have been mentally handicapped or retarded. Both being handicapped gave us something in common. I was not in any way intellectually handicapped – my two 'O' levels were more than around fifty percent of the population would ever get; my brother had left school without any 'O' levels at all. I was still handicapped in other ways that only became apparent during the course at the Rehabilitation Centre; I was more socially handicapped than he was. He talked more than I did and seemed to make friends more easily. I was also more emotionally handicapped, as I was less cheerful and less naturally friendly than he was. Maurice Bridgeland once told me that our emotional development came from and through our relationships with others.

Relations with others have a practical use as much as an emotional use. When we are born, our parents feed and clothe us, keeping us alive. It is only later, after the attendance of practical concerns, that we develop personal relations with people like our parents. At work our relationships with others are more professional than personal, because we are serving a common purpose. The mechanics of social relationships can also be practical when employed through social cognition. I tried telling one man about how I had been treated and how I could not forget. He was busy working and told me that the people who mistreated me were stupid and thus not worth bothering about.

I was called into the social worker's office; it was four weeks since I started the course. She asked me to sit down, and she was as before, seated at her desk. She asked me how I was getting on in the course and if I liked it, to which I replied that I was getting on all right. She said from what she had seen, the reports say: 'He lacks concentration', 'Apathetic', 'Doesn't get on with his job'.

'We don't want to send people out there, without any idea of what they want to do. We don't want to send people out of those gates,' she pointed to the window, beyond which was the entrance to the centre, 'without any idea of what they are good at.'

I was struck dumb the whole time she was talking.

'You've been day dreaming instead of working,' she snapped.

It was as if my worst expectations were coming true. My parents had once discussed my professional future and my father had stated, 'It's not what he wants to do, it's what he can do.' He had continued, 'If it's a physical handicap like an arm missing, we can understand and make concessions to it.' It had long been a fear of mine that being MDDB would hinder any prospect of employment.

'We've been giving you enough rope to hang yourself,' the social worker snarled referring to the four of the six weeks that had passed. 'You would not have lasted half an hour in some jobs.'

AAWV would have said many things if it had been there. The first thing AAWV would have done was combine forces with social cognition, then it would have said, 'It's a question of knowing why I would not have lasted half an hour in some jobs.' By knowing why I would not have lasted half an hour in some jobs, I would be more aware of what I would need to concentrate on.

'You haven't denied what you've been doing,' she snapped. 'Daydreaming, and not working.'

At the time I replied, 'Why would I want to deny it?' I said this because I thought it was true and partly because of my own fears.

'Because if someone didn't deny it, it would cost them their job,' the social worker stated sarcastically. AAWV would have said, 'I would have denied it because it's not entirely true; I was working. You're talking as though I wasn't doing anything at all. I was digging up weeds from the park, and I've been doing office work as opposed to not doing anything.'

Thinking back, the whole atmosphere there was dull, unimaginative and unglamorous; AAWV would have thought to mention this.

'It's your work,' she said, referring to the office work I had been doing.

'Ah,' AAWV would have said, 'you told me I wasn't doing anything at all, now we can see that I was doing something.'

'It's a question of thinking and using what's between your ears,' she went on.

'What word do we associate with concentrate?' AAWV would have asked. If she had sat there dumb, AAWV would have said, 'We associate the word concentrate with the word think. It means we've got to think about what we need to do in a job, any job. By thinking about it and making connections, we form at least a vague idea of what we need to do in a job.'

AAWV (Aggressive Assertive World View) developed around 1990 until 1995. Thinking back to that time, I wanted to tear the social worker apart. Had I done so, I would have done something I would later regret, legally.

'You haven't got a wife and kids to support,' she said, referring to why other men needed employment.

AAWV, together with practical cognitive, would have asked, 'What would I need if I wanted kids?'

If she had hesitated I would have answered the question by saying, 'A wife. What would I need to have a wife?'

If again she had hesitated, 'A girlfriend. What would I need to have a girlfriend?'

If more hesitation, 'The ability to make friends and form relationships.' I would have gone on through AAWV, to tell her how I had my first friend when I was seventeen, and at college.

'When we last met you were thinking about something else.' She meant the experience at South Downs that I could not forget. AAWV would have told her about it. Then I would say that I felt embarrassed about what I had said I wanted to do to him.

I had told her I was out of step with what was going on.

'What do you mean you're out of step?' she questioned.

What AAWV would have said was, 'I am not confident,

that's why I lack concentration, or it may be the other way round. I might lack concentration because I lack confidence. I am not assertive because I am not focused. If I was not producing enough work and being too slow or making too many mistakes you can tell me that. That's instead of telling me I was not doing any of the work at all. You're concerned with a worker's practical needs, like housing, food and wages, but you have no time for more care, or trying to understand things better. It's sad to see a social worker acting the way you have in this office, considering a stereotypical image social workers have, of being too soft.

She had to fill out a form about me.

'Age?' she asked.

'Eighteen,' I replied; she tutted under her breath.

AAWV would have said, 'The way you reacted, tutting under your breath, reflects something. You tutted when I gave you my age, which confirms something that is at the back of my mind. It confirms the fact that daydreaming, to the level I have been, is considered childish. It's one of the things I have been thinking about, along with what people do in jobs. If you were to ask me now what people do in paid jobs, any paid job, I would be able to give you a vague idea. As I said, concentration is related to thinking, and what you would think about someone if they didn't think.' If there had been no answer I would have said, 'If they didn't think, it would infer that they were thick; that would be another thing. I've worked out how other people's minds work, and about what they are thinking.'

The social worker and I eventually got on to discussing jobs. On her desk, there was a box full of cards explaining various occupations; they covered a broad variety. I selected two from the box; one was for an egg packer, the other for a diver; I knew they were odd but only half realised it. When she came back after leaving me alone for a moment, one of the things she mentioned was my choice of jobs.

'These two choices,' she queried, looking at them; 'egg packer and diver indicate you don't seem to have a very realistic idea of what occupation you want.'

AAWV would have said, 'They are too remote from each other, if that's what you mean.'

At one point in the interview, she said in frustration, 'You've always come here on time.' That was true, it was one of the few things I was aware of and would have agreed with, but she went on, 'If you can't carry out the simple tasks, how can you expect to carry out the complicated tasks?'

AAWV would have replied, 'I would only agree with that if you gave me an example of the simple tasks. I was doing the simple tasks, like digging weeds out of the compound and copying out work in the office,' and then gone on to remind her, 'I've got two 'O' levels; it's there on my file, and I've got a good grasp of general knowledge. I'm just not very practical and I'm very slow in certain things. Is the real problem that I'm not working towards a certain standard?'

I did manage to ask her how she knew I was daydreaming. She told me it was because she had been watching me out in the compound whilst I was digging up the weeds. She then treated me to a demonstration of how I apparently looked and acted. She stared upwards into space, looking from side to side in an impression of someone totally lost. I'm sure the impression was exaggerated, as I cannot really imagine myself looking from side to side, especially in such an aimless manner. It was not how I had seemed on the video at the counsellor's office at college. Social cognitive would have been concerned if what she said were true because it made me look as if I acted very oddly.

Finally, the social worker asked me my name, which I gave, then she said, 'Bill, let's be more positive. Think to yourself, I'm going to do the job. I can do the job and I'm going to work.' She led me outside delivering these words and left me in the corridor.

At the time I was too MDDB to be independent-minded and to properly perceive others. I thought other people knew more than me and had more experience than me, which in a sense, most of them did. They did not have to be any more intelligent than me, they just had to be more mentally focused and less inclined to dance around in their living room, run everywhere and laugh to themselves.

There had been a girl there at the centre I had been attracted to; I may even have been in love with her. The trouble was that I showed my attention in an extreme way; I followed her around Cosham whenever I saw her there. I was attracted to her but did not think; I did not realise I was following her. What I also did not realise was the negative effect on her.

I should have tried talking to her more, such as in the centre or somewhere. She was a pretty girl but very shy and difficult to talk to. I now know that if in the past, I had spent more time with people my own age and talked to them, it would have helped me to focus. It might also have helped prevent incidents like me following the girl around and help me to think more about my relationships with others – how I talk to others and what I actually do; the way I walk, dress and act. The way I act refers to things like following the girl around and saying excuse me when I push past people – physical behaviour. Had I been able to do this, it would have helped me relate to other people.

The following two weeks were desperate for me. I had

been shocked by what the social worker had said, and gone home distraught and worried; she had told me that shocks like that were good for some people. I had told the social worker that I was worried about what had happened and about being 'out of step'. She told me not to worry, just to get on with the job. I was so worried that I had gone back to South Downs College and seen my old student counsellor. I told him what had happened and how it confirmed what I feared. I had some time left, two weeks to be exact, but did not know if I could catch up in time. My old student counsellor gave a slight smile, 'You'll catch up Bill,' was all the counsellor could say.

I was dropped from the course early in the sixth week. As a send-off we had a seminar on job hunting. There were a half dozen other blokes who had failed to find anything on the course. I asked the man presenting the seminar if I had shown any improvement.

'There's been no reports from any of the instructors about any dramatic change.' He told me I could come back to the centre when I had the right attitude.

AAWV imagined me saying to him what I could have said to the social worker, that 'I was working.'

After leaving the course the experience began to sink in and I began to develop greater initiative. The initiative was part of my thinking, which made it thinking in itself. Initiative in a work situation enabled me to recognise what had to be done to achieve a task, to recognise that something had to be done properly and it gave me the ability to think for myself without asking others. In terms of concentration, it was not so much what I did think as to what I did not think. That was something I could have told the counsellor and the social worker.

The Employment Rehabilitation Centre was for people who were generally intelligent. I, by comparison, was generally more intelligent than most and as a result, the tasks I had been given were repetitive and dull for me. Subconsciously I got bored with them.

A few weeks after I was dropped from the course, I received a letter from the DHSS. It said my benefits were suspended due to the circumstances of my employment being terminated. Maurice wrote to them, telling them of my autistic tendencies, he also said that now, with a lot of work and motivation, I had achieved two 'O' levels. My benefit continued after a while.

Maurice mentioned autistic tendencies. I do not know how autistic I am now but I suspect I was more autistic then than I am now. I knew I was mentally deaf, dumb and blind, which was really another way of describing my autism. I did not understand the implications of someone being described as autistic, I only knew that it was something I had as a 'problem'. It was something wrong about me that I could not define. Part of the problem was that I could not properly measure my behaviour against other people's. I knew that in the past, my behaviour was odd and it continues to be so up until the present. I felt sorry for myself because of it, yet refused to naturally believe it about myself.

Chapter 11

YTS

The next thing my parents suggested for me was the YTS (Youth Training Scheme). I was now nineteen and should have been too old, but because I had never worked, allowances were made for me.

The placement I gained was at Portsmouth College of Art. I had an interview with the head of Art & Design, and then met the caretaker. He was an ex-Navy man who, to my pleasant surprise, got me started straight away, sweeping corridors and mopping afterwards.

I was working with three other men, one called Sid and two others, both called Dave. I worked there for a year; working on an unpaid training scheme made me content. At the time, I felt I was building my confidence. It did not occur to me where the training scheme was leading or what I was there for or whether it would lead to full-time employment. I was happy that I was actually doing a job – of sorts. I felt angry about what had happened at the rehabilitation centre; I even felt like going back and telling them I was doing a full-time work placement – I wanted to give them a piece of my mind! My mother had persuaded me against it and convinced me that I was actually very dreamy during the time I was there.

My training scheme advisor was a young woman called Melanie Morrit who was very attractive. I once asked her age, out of curiosity and apologised afterwards. My father, on hearing this, had said that I might need the help of the people she represented, so it was best not to offend them.

The problem of the memory of South Downs College still remained with me; I had attended a sociology class as part of the YTS when I started crying. My sociology teacher had spoken to me afterwards, upon learning what had happened, he expressed sympathy.

During this time, I was practising martial arts. Maurice had suggested karate as a way of releasing any pent-up anger and learning to defend myself. My parents had scouted around looking for a karate school and had eventually found one in Portsmouth, at St. Mary's school, opposite the church. It was an interest suggested to me, rather than one that had occurred to me and I took it up in an attempt to help myself deal with all the anger I still felt from over the years, and agreed with Maurice that it could make for a release. All my life I had wanted an interest. Part of the trouble may have been that I could not decide which interest I wanted and as a result, had to have the decision made for me.

I was awkward with karate for a while, partly because I was new to it and partly because I was not very well co-ordinated physically, which may have been due to my problems in estimation and mental agility.

I left karate after five months to take up kung fu and because I disliked the karate instructor; I think I was too sensitive at the time to like him. He was insensitive and sometimes said things that made me feel uneasy; I did not find him very approachable. I even went to the unusual length of phoning him to ask if things were aright between us. He was sincere, and told me he had never developed any dislike for me and wished me luck with my kung fu. I went into the front room of our house and sat on the settee and cried and cried, wailing for a few minutes. I had not spent enough time with a broad enough range of people; I had not met and come to accept people of all ages and personality.

I came to think that when people reached a certain age, they just became more tolerant and more approachable and had felt upset when I had approached someone over twenty-eight who did not seem perfect. I later realised this was a very childish thing to think; I did not have much understanding of age and time. At what point does a person come to realise chronological age? When I was fifteen, I did not know, and I still did not know now at nineteen.

One person I did encounter at karate was a bloke I had known at school who had frequently made fun of me when he spoke to me and now responded to me in a strange way; because he had known me at school, he knew I was odd. AAWV might have confronted him with how he acted towards me. It might have said, 'You're nervous of me aren't you, because I seem odd?' and, 'If you think I'm odd now, I used to be a lot odder! I would have gone to Cliffdale if I hadn't gone to Springfield.'

The kung fu was far more enjoyable because the instructor and the students were far friendlier. It was a wonderful opportunity for me to pursue an interest and make friends. For the first time in my life I was discovering something I could add to and work towards, part of a process. My kung fu instructor became pleased with my progress and told me I moved that bit more quickly than the other students. I was still as socially awkward at the kung fu club as I had been at the other places, but I enjoyed it more. Apart from school and college I had not had all that many places to be awkward at.

I practised a kung fu punch while the teacher was demonstrating another technique. At the time we were being filmed; another student stopped me and told me my kung fu punch did not look good. Once, just before training, I had made a remark about the 1985 Bradford stadium fire. My instructor angrily interpreted it as a sick joke. This was all part of the process of being broken into a broader social context.

The kung fu club, along with work, college and even the rambling club were all different situations with people of different ages and backgrounds. In the case of school and college, it was people my own age, younger and older than me. Not only had I become aware of other people and their colourful qualities and characteristics, but I had also become aware of them as both adults and children.

At work, I would occasionally be told that I was lagging behind the others. Eventually, one of the Daves, little Dave, asked me if I had some personal problem. I said no. He asked because my concentration had apparently become very bad. Melanie Morrit had repeated this question to me over the phone; I had been ringing her about something else and she had taken the opportunity to ask me. I was not aware of my concentration being any worse than usual; I had always known it was poor, but did not see the implications of the word concentration.

From the beginning of the course, Melanie had told me that the main aim was to speed me up, and get me to work faster. If I seemed slow, what were the implications of that? Dave and the others told me that they kept having to do corridors, toilets and stairs that I had already done, and that I forgot to take messages. Melanie warned me that I had to improve my concentration or they would have to find something else for me.

Later on, practical cognitive would realise lots of things about caretaking, like making sure corridors were clean, as well as the stairs; making sure that not too much water was used and to mop it up afterwards; not to leave buckets of water in the middle of the corridor for anyone to trip up over. These were all things that practical cognitive would later see as part of an extended world view; practical cognitive would later process the place, the work and the situation. It would resolve the riddle of the college and the job as one aspect of the society I was in, as one part of Portsmouth; one building that made up the city. It would identify what I would later be more aware of.

One time, when I thought I had been working reasonably quickly, the chief supervisor came up to me and asked in a bemused tone, 'What haaaave you been doing?' I did not yet know what was fully required of me in a work situation. I had more initiative and I felt more confident, yet I did not feel what other people felt in a work situation – the feeling of working to the maximum mental and physical potential and doing the most they are capable of.

There was another occasion, which proved the issue was related to social perception. I had been skiving; or rather MDDB was skiving. MDDB had far less sense of perception. The chief supervisor had come into the library where I was sat, reading. It was during work time.

'What's this then?' he breathed. Later at tea break, little Dave had been shocked and outraged.

'Bill!' he said, staring at me. He was angry in part because he toiled himself, so why shouldn't I?

Social cerebral would understand not just the outrage from the supervisor and college, that MDDB was in the library when he should have been working, but also the expectations in a working environment; these were lost on me. Social cerebral would realise that a person is normally judged by how much they achieve in a workplace and also realise that they would be sacked if they neglected these standards. An empathetic 'world view' would have helped to make me confident in a work situation and understand what was required of me, and make me think that 'if they can do it and hold down a job, so can I.' Practical cognitive would later be the key to unlocking the many puzzles in everyday life that were related to jobs.

I enjoyed spending time with my workmates, even though they were a lot older than me. When I was with them, I felt I was learning more about what working people were like.

Aside from the skiving incident, I did not make all that many 'social mistakes' with the lads. I would make endless jokes, most of them the lads would enjoy. I read about a French film from the records in the library that was fairly ridiculous. It was about, I kid you not, a pair of talking knickers. I casually mentioned this to the lads and it brought groans and amusement. It did not seem to strike me as silly to mention it, I just did. I did not appreciate how they might react.

I once ate in the college library. I sensed that eating lunch in the library amongst all the books might upset someone but did not fully realise it. Little Dave heard about it and told me the head of department would have my balls for breakfast. I knew I could not eat in the libraries at Cosham or Commercial Road. The college had both a library and a canteen. This may have confused me as to what was acceptable in this college setting; it was also a question of practical consideration. Practical cognitive would have realised that food eaten in the library would lead to greasy, dirty fingers that in turn would lead to dirty books through handling.

I once happened to be in one of the art classrooms. Out of curiosity, I looked through some of the books they had on comic strips and drawings. I casually mentioned this to my colleagues and they reacted very strongly, telling me none of us were supposed to do that. We were only supposed to clean the college; I would later realise this without it being explained. There were no rules laid down when I first started going into the classrooms and reading the books. For a caretaker, I now realise it was basically not done. It may have seemed odd, opening books in the first place – I felt it was similar to me reading the *Time* magazines in the library at South Downs and how that seemed odd. I had done it simply on a whim. It was no more 'done' than a caretaker going into the classroom of a school, and reading history books.

I only talked occasionally to the students. There was a time I was in a newsagent's shop near the college. I saw the face of a particularly beautiful actress on the front cover of a woman's magazine. I took the magazine down and started flicking through it to the article on the said actress. There were some students standing nearby, whom I became aware of as they began to saunter out of the shop. I told one of them I was looking through the magazine for an article on the beautiful actress. I must have realised what I was doing and tried to dispel my embarrassment. It backfired on me towards the end of term when I got barracked with a cascade of jeers from a group of lads; it happened as I entered the canteen. This was followed by one of them mentioning the name of the beautiful actress as they got up to leave. If I had known the effect my actions would have, I would not have done what I did, especially not in view of the fact there were other people in the newsagent's.

The YTS ended without any sign of a job. I attended an interview with a careers advisor who discussed with me what I wanted to do next. He told me he knew about the problems I had, that had been caused by my treatment at South Downs. He gave me a long speech about how he had been badly treated but had risen above it. He told me whatever job I did, I would have to concentrate, even if it was a simple job like sweeping the floor and that I would have to get any task done in a certain time.

My college, on hearing that I was leaving, asked me what sort of thing I would like to do, for example gardening, building, joining the services etc. I said a job telling people what to do. By this, I meant a job advising people on things, in other words a counselling job.

'Are you sure people would react well to being told what to do, Bill?' the advisor asked. I had not stated my intention properly. It was also general ignorance of the choice of job itself.

Chapter 12

Closure

The trouble caused by the bullying at South Downs sorted itself out. It was in the middle of the year. I had been looking for one of the two students, the smaller one. For some reason I hated him in particular. It was not just the way he had treated me but also the way he looked and seemed generally. I still tended to judge people by first impressions and appearance. I called him 'Rat face', because I remember him as being rat faced; I regarded him as a freak, someone or something that did not fit in with my ideal impression of society.

In one session with Maurice, we had discussed my problem of not knowing how 'people work'. Maurice had compiled a list of things with another person who had my problem and showed it to me. There were not supposed to be any rules to how people behaved but Maurice and the other bloke had established a set of governing factors. The first governing factor or 'rule', was that everybody is different. The second 'rule' was not to judge by appearances. These are the only two rules I remember. The one about not judging by appearances was one I found difficult to apply to my own thinking.

Maurice was very interested in me calling the student 'Rat face'. He saw it as a focusing of my feelings. I had gone back to college to look for the student. I did not find him but I found two other technical block students who might know him. He lived in Leigh Park and I rang him up. I asked about 'Rat face', or rather the name I had been given. The person on the other end said they knew him. I was now in two minds about 'Rat face'. I knew where to find him but did not know whether to directly confront him. Later I was to realise the implications of a person behaving the way I did, both morally and socially.

It was about a week later; I had been drinking in Uncle Tom's Cabin at the top of Cosham. I was walking home up Burrill Avenue when someone called out to me from a car that was parked beside the pavement. I stopped to look at the person who had shouted; it was one of two blokes sitting in the front. At first I mistook him for someone I knew at Springfield.

'Do you remember us? We used to go around as a group,' he said.

'Did you go to Springfield?' I asked.

He looked dumb, 'What's Springfield?' Then, 'We were at the same college as you when someone slashed your tyres. You were looking for that person, weren't you?'

'Do you know who it was?' I asked.

'Yeah,' he replied. 'It was me.' I turned round and started walking home, up Burrill Avenue. The car came over the road to the side I was now walking on.

'We're going to run you over,' he shouted up at me. The car drove closer.

'Come here,' he said. If I had been able to judge his intentions I would not have walked back to the car. I was standing a few inches from the car facing the window, the bloke leant out, swearing, then without warning tried to punch me. He did not strike quite quickly enough and I dodged the punch easily. I remember thinking that this person has punched me, or has tried to punch me. I knew that in this situation it was acceptable for me to punch back, so I did. I had done what a lot of people would have done by hitting back I thought to myself. I turned and started to walk up the Avenue again.

I had my back to them when they attacked. The bloke I hit had got out of the car, along with the bloke next to him. I thought, 'Right, I'm going to be attacked.' I offered no resistance, and had my eye kicked repeatedly. It became black and blue and puffed up. My glasses were stamped on by the other bloke and broke. My dad took me to the hospital upon seeing me stagger in, confused and bloody; I was trying to remember the last twenty minutes. My eye had to endure eleven stitches at the hospital.

When I got back, my mother and brother berated me for what they thought I had brought upon myself.

'It'll be a lesson to you,' my mother said.

My brother said, 'It goes to show, don't stir up the plebs.'

I was lying on my bed, face down, when I heard this. I had not anticipated people enough to judge my own decisions; I did not know enough about people to interpret how certain people would react and behave.

I was forced to go back to my kung fu classes with a swollen black eye; it was embarrassing. When my work colleagues saw it, they asked me why I didn't use my kung fu. The reason was that it didn't occur to me at the time. My thoughts had not been organised enough to remember what I had learnt; maybe I could not apply what I did in one situation to what happened in another. I did not use my kung fu because I did not even think of fighting back. I had not learnt to react instinctively to situations that demanded it. Later, as I learnt more kung fu it had more time to sink in and I felt that I could react instinctively, if the situation required it. My body and brain could automatically act as one.

My kung fu teacher and I became friends. He told me he had a number of 'A' levels and urged me to try for some myself. He said going for 'A' levels was like martial arts, in that a person could do it if they believed they could do it. He asked me what 'A' levels I would be interested in and what career they might be for? I considered this and said I wanted to be a Barrister. The reason for this was not because of my interest in law or any earlier ambitions to pursue a legal career, it was because of a TV series I had seen and followed, called the *Paper Chase*. I had liked the scenes of the law students in the classroom and had been enthralled by the use of legal language. My teacher said he had seen the programme as well and liked it. He told me that I would need to enrol soon.

I enrolled in 'A' Level law at the end of 1984. I felt awkward at first sitting with people I did not know. There was a coloured lad who came up to me while I was seated and started talking to me. A girl student was with him who was also coloured; she started talking to me as well but from what she said, she seemed cold and standoffish.

'I'm from a mental home,' she once said, seated and looking into space. I could not interpret statements like this and all their implications; I just imagined many statements were flippant and knew that I could not consciously use them myself.

We were given textbooks to study on law; I felt myself being 'sucked into' what the textbooks contained as I sat at home reading them. I felt that once I started reading the words I would not be able to stop, it was as though they would concentrate all my thoughts in one place. In the future, concentrating all my thoughts in one place and at one time would be something I would experience and need, but in this case, the feeling was too tremendous and too much too soon.

I would spend time peering at a page in the textbook, deciding whether to read it properly or not. I built up a lot of energy through restlessness and worry, and as usual, I expended it by running round the block in the area I lived. I had often wandered around the block in the past, for the same reason: to use up my energy. I had no outlet other than that. I had no understanding of any outlet that would not be considered odd by others.

The more I tried to work, the more tired I became. Trying to work meant spending time sitting at the desk in the front room. Maurice had told me the more actual work I did, the less tired I would feel.

I gave up the course and stopped going to law classes. I spent a lot of time watching TV and lolling around, rather than working. My mother was supportive but my father was angry and called me a layabout. Hours were wasted; it was one of the first times I had encountered a situation where my entire mental and emotional self was on the verge of a change. My mind blanked, I could not do anything because I could not think of how to do anything. When I saw Maurice, he asked me to think of all the things I could do; he made a list of things I mentioned, such as buying tapes of music and exploring parts of Portsmouth. I never got round to doing any of these things; instead, I lolled around at home, went to one or two libraries (Commercial Road or Cosham) or wandered around Commercial Road looking in WH Smith's and other bookshops. I also continued looking for work.

Chapter 13

Moth Tail Caterpillar Scheme

*I*n April of that year I went on the 'Moth Tail Catterpillar'
scheme. This was a government sponsored work scheme that
hoped to bring work to the unemployed through community
projects. I attended the opening for the scheme in a room in
the civic offices in the Guildhall with a few other lads. The
opening was a lecture by a large, balding, ex-Navy man with
a moustache, called Nigel Sizer; the talk was more pretentious
than the job itself.

After the lecture, Nigel saw us one by one. When he came
to me, I tried to explain that I had some kind of problem with
communication.

'You mean you're shy?' he said, smiling at me. Earlier
he had said he would come down hard on anyone who made
unkind remarks to a colleague because of any mental handicap
they had.

I began in an area of Portsmouth that was unknown to me. I
had been told to get to the site on time in the morning. I arrived
at a large trailer that I surveyed for a moment, then went up
and knocked on the door. A fairly haggard, middle-aged man
answered it and I asked if he knew anything about the Moth
Tail scheme. He said, 'Oh, another one,' and invited me in.

I was shocked. Inside the shabby looking trailer were
the type of men I had rarely come into contact with before.

They were the scruffiest, most common looking men I had ever seen; they were, I learnt, typical council workers. This experience affected the social cerebral part of my mind, which would later form new opinions because of it. I was shocked by how the men looked and spoke but I did realise after a period of time that they were an example of the sort of men who lived and worked in Portsmouth; I later came to accept them as people.

On the first day I was there we did hardly anything; this was repeated on many other days. I was so nervous and uptight, I had lost my way cycling to the main office. I had gone there to collect my working boots on my first day but had gone the wrong way. When I got back to the trailer, one of the men mentioned to me that I had taken the long way round and that I could have taken a shorter route. I was not relaxed because I was starting a new job, which combined with the sort of men I was mixing with, plus the setting I found myself in, made me less able to take time in deciding which direction to take. This was one example of how I had failed to relax in a social situation. My decisions and physical actions were being dictated by the presence of others.

The job paid £48.00 per week and comprised of five to seven hours a day. The job involved going round spraying the gardens and vegetated areas of Portsmouth, using a poison that actually killed 'cats' (short for caterpillars), as well as weeds. We would work as a group, normally on foot. When we had finished in one area, we would shift the trailer to another site.

There was an amusing incident at the time I was working on the scheme. One weekend I was with my parents visiting some Quaker friends of my mother. The couple were believers in the Buddhist concept that all life, animals or otherwise, was sacred. We were sitting in their garden drinking tea when the wife asked me what I did for a living.

'Oh,' I answered casually. 'I kill cats.' My mother later told me she had been taken aback.

'What, in your garden?' the wife asked.

'No,' I replied. 'In other people's gardens.'

If I had been listening more to what was being said, and had been able to process what I heard, I may have been able to adjust to it. I could have listened to them talk about the Buddhist beliefs that would in turn have affected how I described my occupation, so rather than saying, 'I kill cats', I could have said that I worked on a Government scheme. This would have been more suitable. Or, I could have just said that 'cats' was short for caterpillars, which is was.

I still had difficulty communicating with others due to my mental state. I had always been quiet but had been making progress at the college with the caretaking job; talking and joking with colleagues had helped me come out of myself. Once, at South Downs college, I was sitting in the refectory when the bloke sitting opposite me had called me the master of conversation; he had meant it as irony.

One week after starting on the Moth Tail scheme I came in and a colleague told me, 'I know where you live; St James'.' I asked my mother what St James' was and she said it was a home for the mentally ill. The same person who said this, also said, 'I don't know you, William,' meaning that I had not been communicating enough since I had arrived. This same nuisance, a moustached, largely built man was to bedevil me through the scheme. He probably thought I was being quiet to be deliberately standoffish and remote, snubbing him and the others. Often, I knew what I wanted to say but could not think of the words to use; I wonder what would have been the reaction if I had told the whole group that my being quiet and remote came from being able to blank my mental state because I was studying 'A' level law. I did not have the courage to say this; it did not even occur to me to try to mention this. If I had, I now realise it might have helped. The one who disliked me once became genuinely angry because I did not give him a packet of crisps in return for half a packet of biscuits.

There was also another problem working with the men on the Moth Tail scheme, the problem of not understanding the strong Portsmouth accent. If I had spent more time with blokes and girls at school, I might have understood the Portsmouth accent a bit better. The men seemed to me, to speak to themselves under their breath. Maurice later pointed out that they tended to leave out the ends of words, for example, 'I went to the shops' became, 'I went to the sho'.'

There was one individual who sat on a bucket and wore glasses; I got to know him later. One of the other men, a little man who did most of the talking, had said to me, 'You don't talk much, do you?' I replied that neither did the bloke who sat in the corner.

'Well, he's the Prof,' the man said. The Prof was called the Prof because he wore glasses; his real name was Eric.

I started talking to Eric as I found his accent far easier to understand, he also seemed less rough and more approachable in manner. One of extraordinary things about him was his belief in Nazis. Eric believed that the country's problems could be solved and improved through just one year under Hitler. Having stated this, he then asked me if I wasn't shocked, and was slightly surprised that I wasn't. I was aware of who Hitler was as an historical figure and I knew who the Nazis were, but for some strange reason I could not automatically connect the two. I knew that the Nazis had committed crimes historically but could not whatsoever connect them with

Hitler. When he mentioned Hitler's name, I regarded him as just another dictator. This was in part, an inability to make connections between subjects, as well as my inability to process information properly. Some of the things Eric said later upset me, not because they were hurtful but because they seemed trite and too real. They reflected all the dreary little things that made up everyday life.

Eric had once told me he was forty years old in terms of mental and emotional development, whereas he was in fact nineteen but had been told he was emotionally forty years old by a psychologist. This was because of all the harsh experiences he had gone through such as when his girlfriend left him after three years. AAWV could have used self-knowledge to tell him that if he was emotionally forty, I was about ten. I had not yet properly adjusted to the world and society; if I had developed at all, I must have developed inwards, which was why I hated the sort of things that the Prof had said, things that reflected reality.

I once told Eric that someone had said my trouble was that I knew how lucky I was, but did not know how unlucky I could be. The Prof has said that I did not have any aggression and that I needed to find something I could get my teeth into and then, 'chomp away'. The Prof said this in a casual, cheerful way, which made it feel more painful and annoying later on, because it represented reality and the pain of everyday life. Eric was probably talking about me being so quiet and never expressing any views and opinions; AAWV later developed the confidence to do exactly this, to process and create views and opinions in my head.

The memory of what he said caused me to have tantrums later on. I had asked him what he meant and he'd said getting your teeth into a project of some sort. The projects and interests he mentioned seemed to be about big battles in military history like the battle of Gettysburg and about big battleships, on which he was supposed to be an expert. The world wisdom he expressed, the conscious awareness of society he inhabited, was something I did not share. One of the things I should have said to him at the time was that the things he said hurt me; it sounded like nails on a blackboard.

Are the autistic's nerves more sensitive than other people's? Does the whole mechanism of hearing and feeling function differently for an autistic person?

The effect of some of the things Eric said to me was one of painful frustration. Eric once said he was seventy percent sane, this meant he was thirty percent insane. I could have told him that me being autistic could, through definition and interpretation, make me even less sane. I could also have said that my condition alongside his 30 percent insanity, made us targets for the kind of people he claimed to follow, i.e. the Nazis.

There was time I was out with Eric, wandering the streets of Portsmouth when Eric had looked at a piece of architecture and said he admired it. I said that was a good thing. He asked me why, and I replied because it must mean you know what you want to do when you are older – you want to be an architect. He looked at me, grinned and then laughed. I remember thinking what did I say to cause laughter? What social error had I committed? Then I realised I had said something that had sounded odd. The social part of my mind had not established what I was saying and had not made connections beforehand. It was not aware of social connections. I could have told myself:

1) The situation he mentioned is about some architecture he liked.

2) Then asked myself, does this mean he wants to be an architect?

3) But if after carefully evaluating this information, I didn't know, I could have:

4) asked him.

Or, after Eric had mentioned the architecture he liked, I could have asked, 'Have you ever considered becoming an architect?' The question itself might seem a bit high flown but it was preferable to what I had said.

Eric seemed frustrated with the way I acted; I never complained about the job we were doing, what it entailed, the low wages, the clothes we were given or the boredom. The job was often tedious and we sat around doing nothing quite often. In my case however, I did not have much to compare it with. I was becoming more aware of what most jobs entailed, and in the case of this job it should have entailed more work. The average wage and hours should have been there, but weren't, but I was content with getting more money than I normally did on the dole. I did not need a proper wage as I was living with my parents; accommodation and all my meals were provided for. I was still curious about a proper wage and proper employment though.

Eric was once in a frustrated mood. In the middle of it he asked, 'What's stopping you from having a good swear?' The 'a good', was another realistic piece of language, which along with 'chuffed', grated on me as something meaninglessly street-wise. It caused me pain and frustration; social cognitive would have said that swearing depends on social circumstances and what the social situation is. If a person is in a situation where everyone else swears it is more acceptable for him or her to swear. If a person is in a situation where everyone, for certain reasons, does not swear then it is not acceptable for him or her to swear.

Eric said he had been going out with a girl for three years;

he would have experienced this between the ages of sixteen to nineteen. I could have said I was seventeen before I had a friend my own age. I could also have said that I was emotionally around ten years old at twenty-one years of age, compared to his being emotionally forty when he was nineteen.

We had once been going from house to house asking people if they wanted their garden sprayed for caterpillars; I had to remember what to say, 'Hello. I am from Portsmouth City Council and we wondered if….' Eric was alongside me patiently trying to help me with what I had to say; he had once told me I lacked aggression. AAWV would have told him that I needed something to do that would stimulate me and make me think, rather than that I lacked aggression.

Halfway through the scheme I went on holiday to Scotland and by the end of my holiday, I had met people, done a lot of walking and horse riding. I felt I had changed from how I had been over the last year. Maybe it was down to the break in routine from what I normally did and a break from where I normally was; the holiday helped me to relax with people. I trusted the people I met in Scotland more than the men on the Moth Tail scheme and felt more relaxed and far less intimidated by them. The holiday had provided me with something the job on the scheme had not. I had travelled to another part of Britain providing change from where I normally was in Portsmouth. There had also been a relief from my established routine.

At the end of the holiday, one of the girls who had been with me told me I had changed from when she first met me. She also told me I needed to get out more.

When I got back, I found I was still remote and distant from my workmates, all except Eric. I got on reasonably well with most of them except the moustached, largely built man; he was the one who had originally disliked me for not talking to anyone. I could understand him disliking what he saw, and my lack of friendliness, but some of what he said and did, hurt. Perhaps I should have told him that I was quiet because of my autism and the problems that created. He seemed to sense there was something wrong with me.

There was the remark about me living in a mental home as well as another incident when we went into a community centre after doing a job. Some of us were sitting down, others were playing billiards or darts. The man, I shall call Chris, was sitting next to me while I was listening to the jukebox; there was a girl talking to us. She suddenly she started laughing so I turned to see why, only to see Chris with his tongue flapping out of his mouth and his eyes unfocused as though he was dead. I tried ignoring him. I was eating a chocolate bar. Chris went on, imitating my actions and I realised he was making fun of me for seeming odd, mad or somehow handicapped. I was hurt because it was something I had always suspected about myself. It seemed he was attacking me personally and I was only half aware of it.

I looked hurt and Chris picked up on it. I looked hurt in part to deliberately create some sympathy from my tormentor but Chris just said, 'I've upset him now!' All it did though, was make Chris think that I was mentally handicapped, as that was how a mentally handicapped person might react. He may have suspected it anyway because of my body language and facial expressions.

Maurice said that Chris was more socially aware than I was but that was obvious, as a lot of people were more socially aware than I was. Chris may have known that mentally handicapped people felt sensitive about their condition, a condition that made them vulnerable.

The most talkative member of the group and its natural

leader had told me I had a new nickname; it was Planet. Planet, the man said, was Greek for wanderer and I had got the nickname because I wandered round outside the trailer.

I was using the spare time I had to look for another job. I had been told that I was slow in doing the actual work on the scheme. I would take more time than usual spraying a tree or a bush and I had difficulty estimating how long it would take me to do things. I could not balance doing it quickly with not overlooking things, or making mistakes. One time I was temporarily put with another group; I had been sitting outside the trailer at break time. The leader had loudly mentioned to the others that I was a gormless sod who was always grinning to himself. That hurt me, but grinning to myself was a habit that had been with me since as far back as I can remember, since I was five or six. It was just something I did and had always had trouble with.

There were other incidents with this group; the group's leader had asked me if I was on drugs. I was very shocked with him asking me this question but later realised that he was referring to the bright, unfocused expression in my eyes. It was the same expression the social worker at the Employment Rehabilitation Centre had exaggerated and the same expression familiar in a lot of autistic people, as though they see things but did not compute what they see.

When I first started with the other group, Eric had taken me to a part of the site, away from the main area and showed me something that amused him.

'That sums up this job,' he said, pointing down. It was a council worker, a girl, curled up on a pile of wooden boards, sleeping. I was very tired and I thought this example gave me carte blanche to copy her, the only problem was, I was in full view of the other workers and the new team leader. I had not realised that because the girl could not be seen, she did not have any effect on other people's thinking. I was half slumped over an oil drum, eyes closed, and half asleep when I was woken by voices.

'Oi, mate! Butlins is up the road there.'

Next time, if I did sleep, it would be out of sight of anyone.

Chapter 14

Clocking on with Reliance

I applied for a job with a security firm, called Reliance. We had a conference in the main space in the Commercial Road job centre. I was still very tense and mentally confused, which showed at the introductory talk for the job. The manager of the company had told us we would be required to work shifts. I understood shifts, but I did not understand what the job would entail, in terms of the work that actually needed to be done.

We were all seated in one corner of the job centre, being addressed by Hefin Thomas, the company's manager. He was talking to the whole group of applicants when he stopped and asked me if I had anything to say; he must have noticed how remote and quiet I seemed.

'Do you employ dogs?' I asked, without thinking. I had posed the question in the wrong way. I could have asked, 'Do you use dogs?'

Hefin understood what I meant, but he answered the actual question with, 'If they can fill out the application forms, yes.' This caused lots of laughter. It was a slip of the tongue where I had substituted one word for another, thus changing the whole meaning of the question. If I had been more mentally agile, I would have been able to ask a better question in the few seconds available.

The introductory talk at the job centre was followed

by another, longer talk at the company centre in Totton, Southampton. We were given talks on security procedures such as cleaning the site and doing rounds. There were things however that I could not understand, things of a more simple nature, such as what the job was.

If I had been aware of basic social factors, I had neither remembered nor built on them. This is something that would normally occur at an early age when society and parents first explain the practical and immediate facts of everyday life to children. It is the reason why children's programmes feature articles on for example, factories and mines. I, on the other hand, could not immediately understand what this, or any job demanded. I knew Reliance was a security firm and that I would be employed as a security guard but I could not imagine who they worked for. Was it for one company, the government, more than one company? I had no idea who night need us, and for what.

I was given a uniform, the jacket of which was too big for me, and was assigned to a site called Fraser Battery, which was a naval base in a remote part of Portsmouth, besides the sea, opposite Eastney. The bloke who showed me the ropes was called Dave Paine. The site, I was told, was a naval gun range. I first met Dave outside a small square building, which was attached to a larger building, beside a barrier next to the entrance. Dave showed me all the places at the site where there were keys. There was a clock we took with us that we fitted the keys into then turned to mark them. These journeys round the site were called patrols. The first time, Dave took me round, the second time I had gone round unaccompanied but forgot the take the clock. Dave said something to me that I did not hear properly and soon forgot.

From the beginning, my mental state caused me the same

problems with colleagues that the Moth Tail Caterpillar scheme had; I was still very quiet. I now know things I could have said to Dave Paine to be more communicative. I could have talked about what I had done, discussed how my last job compared with this present one. AAWV would be a lot better at understanding the situation, but all I had then was MDDB. The state I had been in over the year had been due to my experience with 'A' level Law. It had been partly of my own creation, coming about due to barricrs that I had subconsciously put up in my head.

I learnt later that Dave Paine thought I was thick because I forgot to take the clock with me to do the patrol. I had observed what he had done when he showed me but I had not been able to make the connection between him showing me, and what I had to do. It had been a mistake I made on a simple aspect of the job.

Because of my quiet, remote nature and the clock incident, I was not considered totally reliable. They still did not know what to exactly make of me and only allowed me to do nights at Fraser Battery. I was called a 'dreamy daisy' by Hefin Thomas. He told me that other senior officers had wanted to sack me early on but that he had persuaded them to give me another chance. I had hoped my concentration would improve, but it did not.

Before commencing what would be a long time at Fraser's, I went to the racing track at Goodwood to provide security there. I was one of a team of four men, including Dave Paine and a younger man. There was also an older man, as one of the team, who, on my second shift, treated me badly. He started nagging me about the state of my shoes compared with his. He told me mine were dirty and put his shoes alongside them to show just how much cleaner his were. AAWV would have said that my shoes were just worn. The man, Hazell, verbally attacked me all through the shift at the racetrack. He attacked my personality, and told me I would be a pain in the arse to someone. At first I asked if he had any rank; he claimed that he was a supervisor. AAWV would later realise I could have rung up the central office at Totton, Southampton and asked if this was true; they could have checked through their records. At the time I did not have the initiative to think of something like that; I was still quite MDDB, mentally deaf, dumb and blind.

I got upset during the shift, not just because of Hazell's haranguing but also because of the feeling it induced – of not being able to do things. Hazell had once called me before him and told me that I was useless. I threw up in the toilets over the course of the weekend. AAWV would have defended me on several points. It would have demanded to know what I was doing wrong, and in specific detail. All Hazell kept telling me was that I kept mucking up.

A few days later I was back at my usual job on the gatehouse at Fraser Battery. The rules of the job meant there was always another guard with me, so there would be one guard at the gate while the other did a patrol. I could not yet do things too challenging; I knew some things about the job but not enough. I could not collect and retain enough facts to then process.

AAWV and practical cognitive would have realised what I needed to do and think about while doing day shifts. People came in and I needed to stop them if I did not recognise them. For every person that came on site, I needed to photograph them into my mind after checking their identity. After that, I needed to remember their faces and compare them to any faces I did not know.

I worked with several other blokes in the course of the shifts. One of the blokes was called Mark Hawk. While we were sitting in the guardhouse, he told me he believed in a relationship that was socially open to a point where individuals could express their most personal details, whether sexual, emotional or mental. This applied for example, as to whether a person was gay or not.

'I'm not gay,' he stated bluntly. He directly asked me if I was gay, and I, in all honesty, denied it. He mentioned a man he knew who had been gay while working with Reliance. He had left to become a riding instructor. I made a joke about him riding side-saddle.

'That's nasty,' Mark said with a gentle smile. Social cognitive would have prevented me from making the remark or alternatively made me consider what I was saying, before I made it.

Mark complained about someone stealing the food he kept in the fridge at the gatehouse. I asked what a security guard would do if another security guard was stealing food from him.

'Well, what do you think?' He looked at me, large-eyed and surprised, as though I should have understood. 'He'd punch you in the face.'

Social cognitive would have understood the implications of that in more detail.

I mentioned Hazell and how he had treated me at Goodwood.

'Ron Hazell? Oh, he's the least of anyone's problems,' Mark replied nonchalantly.

I was surprised.

'You mean he's not a supervisor?'

'Oh, he's not anything. He's an ordinary security guard like you and me.'

Mark Hawk was sacked later for going home too early.

I was now almost on my own at the gatehouse. There was

Chuck Heard, an ex-naval captain and Duke Dampier, a small young man. A lot of my nights were now spent with either of these two men. Chuck Heard once told me that Dave Paine had hated me; it must have been because I had been so quiet and thus had disturbed Dave. Mark Hawk had once said that Dave could be quite thick skinned.

There was a time I was called down to Cosham railway station to be picked up to go to a different site. I needed to wait ten minutes and in those ten minutes, when I was waiting by the railway, a group of three teenage girls wandered up to me and started verbally attacking me. This made me angry, I kept asking myself in my mind why they were doing this. They would wander off then come back again.

One of them standing on her own said, 'My friend tells me you work with spastics.' That was the breaking point for me; they could say whatever they wanted but not about any mental problem I had or anything else that might make me different from others.

This is what I thought the first girl was saying: that I was a spastic. I seized her arm the moment she said this. She got scared and went off to get her friend, the fattest in the group. I did not know myself what spastic meant but thought it meant someone whose disability made them different from other people. I had not yet realised disability in more diverse forms or its difference from illness.

The girl came back a few seconds later with her fat friend who demanded, 'Did you try to hit my friend?'

I told her I had got hold of her friend's arm.

'Did you do it because she asked you if you worked with spas...' she stopped before saying the word she knew had had an effect. I went over to a nearby public toilet across from the railway. As I walked there they screamed, 'Spastic! Spastic!'

I was very hurt by being called a spastic. It seemed it had finally happened; I was abused for being different from others by being a spastic or 'Dinlow'.

AAWV would have dealt with the situation by not swearing at them or being abusive back. That was all MDDB could think to do at the time in order to defend myself.

From the moment the situation started, AAWV would have said, 'Pardon? Excuse me, but the way you are talking to me is rude. I was just standing here, minding my own business when you started being rude.' AAWV would have stated the situation. AAWV could have incorporated a broader social viewpoint.

'A lot of people would consider it rude to come up to someone and start swearing at them, as well as odd.' If they had continued in their frenzied way, which they did, AAWV would have carried on talking to them, lecturing them in a serious tone. AAWV would have been more assertive than MDDB.

When I was called a spastic, AAWV would have asked, 'Do you know what that means? It means someone with Cerebral Palsy. Cerebral Palsy means their bodies don't respond to their brains properly. If you knew that, you would be careful how you used the words.' Then mischievously, 'Cerebral Palsy would be big words for you to use. They have got too many syllables.' MDDB could only desperately think of, 'Why don't you piss off back to your broken homes?' This would cause more anger and have no real effect; MDDB had been scared of the girls in the first place. The girls were of course, part of a group that were poor, lower class and ignorant – apart from the rest of society. They were violent and dangerous; MDDB labelled people like this.

I asked them, through their taunts, whether they were

attracted to me or whether they were genuinely trying to upset me. They referred to the latter that they were genuinely trying to upset me. AAWV would have been braver, and said what it wanted to say, despite who it was talking to or whether it could be understood. It would have said that I had two 'O' levels when they called me stupid. It would have remembered that I had two 'O' levels and logically applied this fact to support the argument that I was intelligent. AAWV might also have said something very insulting to one or two of the girls. When one of them said, 'Are you going to drag us up that alleyway and rape us?' It would have said, 'Have you ever been raped? If you have, you would know all about it. If you haven't, be careful how you talk about it.'

Once, when I had been on the Moth Tail scheme I had asked Ernie what I should say to the other blokes when I was with them. Ernie was surprised and had replied, 'Say whatever you want to say.'

AAWV made me less shy and free to express myself, however, what a person says has to be pre-meditated, meaning they need to evaluate what they want to say and its effect before they say it. AAWV would have tried reasoning with the girls, talking to them in a particular way about it. MDBB would have not tried talking to the girls in a practical way about particular things, as it thought they might not understand.

AAWV would have understood that the people it was dealing with were not worth bothering about anyway. That attitude may have been useful the rest of the time but for ten minutes I was trapped in one situation that I was obliged to deal with. The attitude that they were not worth bothering about would have been shared by a lot of people. It was an attitude AAWV would have recognised and empathised with.

It was what I heard from people afterwards about the girls,

and for that matter about the students at college; the girls seemed to epitomise pure evil.

There was another bloke from the group of young people near to them who stood near me and started to talk.

We talked about where we were lived and then he asked suddenly, 'How old are you?'

I said, 'Twenty-two.'

He then said, 'Hey,' presumably to the girls. 'Leave him alone.' I assumed all the girls were younger than twenty-two, as I tended to think, as my brother did, that people's behaviour tended to change with age and that they became more stable and responsible as they grew up.

After ten minutes of this fracas my father came down in his car to pick me up. As we drove off one of the girls kicked my father's car.

When I got back home I was practically shaking; I had never realised people could be like that. I had been trying to tell them to go over there, to a side of the railway crossing and away from me for ten minutes – out of desperation. One of the girls had told me to stand on the track and wait for a train to go over me. AAWV would have made the retort 'I would stand there to get away from you!'

After all this, I found out I had gone to the wrong place to be picked up. I was certain they had said the railway crossing, but was wrong – it was outside my house. I had to talk to someone about the experience as it was very traumatic.

The next shift I did was with Mark Hawk; as usual, he was too distant to talk to properly. I briefly mentioned my trouble with the girls; I just heard him say, 'The girls are the worst.'

My next shift was with Allen Pegg. I mentioned what had happened to him.

'Did you have any trouble with girls?' I asked him.

'No,' he replied, thinking I meant sex. 'Just find them and fuck 'em.'

I repeated the question, describing what had happened and finally Allen said, 'Oh, what did you do?'

'Nothing,' I said.

'What would I have done?' he asked half to himself. 'I would have torn them apart, that's what I would have done!' This was a surprise to me, and a revelation.

'What would you have said?' Allen went on to describe how he would have insulted and humiliated the girls completely. He would have said things in an aggressive manner that I tried to imitate. After two or three attempts Allen said I almost had it.

He said he could get really nasty in retaliation.

'There are lots of things you can say to a woman,' he pointed out. These were all the things that made me feel more powerful, after all these years of being dominated by this sort of person. I mentioned this to Allen.

'You mean you would have just hit them, or felt like hitting them?' I asked, bemused.

'I wouldn't have needed to hit them. I would have just ripped them apart. I'll be damned if I'm going to let a woman speak to me like that.' He seemed almost angry that I had not been more aggressive, disregarding the fact I was deeply shaken. 'You let them get away with how they spoke to you.' He would later cite this as evidence of my lack of aggression, verbal in this case rather than physical.

Later on, I would be appalled and embarrassed at what Allen had said, almost as much as I had been hurt and scared by the girls; Allen Pegg seemed to resent women abusing him more than men. I had subconsciously known most women were weaker than men, and that this posed no physical threat to most men. I knew this practical fact but I did not feel it in a way that empathised with men like Allen Pegg. I had told Allen that I was surprised by how he had reacted, considering how long I had been abused by girls, through school and elsewhere.

That most women are physically weaker than most men is a practical fact. It was most possible that because I could not process practical facts as well as abstract facts, I could not compare them with socially cognitive facts. I could not connect or compare the fact of women being weaker, with how Allen Pegg and other men like him might feel about being abused by them. I had not yet worked out that it might actually damage their egos.

The whole experience would gradually change me, as though something had been shaken up by the whole thing. Encountering hardship like this may have stimulated change in me.

I encountered the girls a few more times in and around Cosham; the numbers diminished to the one fat girl. The experience had planted a seed for something that would grow and expand into something else. My social understanding was still in its infancy.

On one shift with Mark Hawk, a supervisor came round to Fraser's to talk to me. He told me that Allen Pegg had told him how I had cried and broke down when Allen questioned me. The supervisor invited me to relax and express all my feelings; Mark Hawk had casually called the supervisor 'the company shrink'. I knew the remark was coming, the point being I had anticipated it – Mark Hawk had stated his belief about being able to express personal facts to someone. I asked the supervisor, Dave, about my problems with the job and Dave said that a lot of people thought I wasn't taking it all in.

I could have said that, as it occurred to me it wasn't just a question of taking it all in, it was a question of processing the information after taking it in, by which I meant thinking about it. MDDB had prevented me from doing this. MDDB had always seemed like a barrier between myself and who or what was around me. It was that, or it was something – a mechanism not yet developed, a system of thought – that had not come about through any system of thought.

This absence of any proper system of thought had prevented me from analysing and understanding my job at Fraser's. I had not been able to do things like remember faces because I had not been able to absorb and process the information. I told Dave the same thing I had told Mark Hawk, that I was not supposed to be able to understand people. Mark Hawk had kept saying, as far as he was concerned, I just did not have any confidence. Dave seemed a bit puzzled by what I claimed to be lack of social understanding.

After both he and Mark Hawk had pondered this, Dave recalled an incident when he had visited the Fraser site at another time. I was with a guard called Dave Damper. Dave Damper had been upset because the company had been giving him too many hours to do; all the shifts had been interfering with his private life to the extent he had not been able to attend a relative's funeral. Dave Damper had been distraught when talking to Dave the supervisor.

Dave the supervisor recalled him knowing I was about to say something; it was by the way my mouth was moving and my general body language. I had said Dave Damper would need a day off to attend the funeral. Dave said that Dave Damper had become even more distraught at this. Mark Hawk seemed to dismiss the fact from his mind.

I said at a later date that the incident with Dave Damper

was rather too odious. I knew it would sound insensitive what I had said, but had not known definitely for certain. I would have told both Dave and Mark Hawk that my learning disability caused me to act as though I was unintelligent when dealing with people. I would have cited the incidents with Mark Hawk when I had made certain remarks, such as the one about the gay, ex security guard riding sidesaddle, or when I asked what a security guard would do if he discovered his food was being stolen.

The first time I had a shift with Mark Hawk I admitted I was afraid of the dark. I had completed my first patrol round Fraser's on my first night shift and because I had got tired as the night wore on, I had started imagining frightening things in the dark. Mark Hawk told me it was something I should do something about. He also told me when I asked him why, that if I did not, it would hold me back. I later imagined it was something about being afraid of the dark in particular that he thought had to be overcome, more than my other fears.

I would have said at the time that in some part of my mind, social cognitive was telling me that being afraid of the dark was more serious than other fears. I might have posed the question whether this was the case and if so, did Mark and other people take this view – was there some social value that deemed being afraid of the dark childish, or was it a social value that condemned all fear?

I had told Mark on the first shift that I had been studying law and given it up. He had asked me why. From his tone of his voice, I had later wondered if there was any sense of reproach, as though there was a social value in him and others that valued success and achievement.

There was another person at Fraser's I worked several shifts with; he was an ex ship's captain, in his late fifties, called

Buck Jones. There was one shift when I was about twenty minutes late. Because I was twenty minutes late, he had to stay on and could not leave the site; in a way, I had reneged on an agreement we made, because he had come twenty minutes early for me.

When I got to the site, late, he was very angry and gave me a haranguing lecture about responsibilities. I got vexed and frustrated throughout; eventually, in a moment of hurt and desperation I tried to defend myself by saying I was often confused and blurted out that I had a mental age of ten. Buck Jones stopped talking and sat down staring at me. I had literally not known what I was saying. I told Buck it was something that I could only sum up about myself; at the time my mental age, once I came to know more about mental ages, was not ten, it was twenty-one exactly.

When I was ten years old, my mental age may well have been higher than ten years since I was frequently reading science books. My emotional age, which is what I meant to say to Buck, was probably about ten. Even thinking about what I had said made me feel embarrassed; I became embarrassed when I realised the impact it would have on other people's thoughts of me.

When I rang Maurice Bridgeland up from the site and told him what I had said, even he seemed slightly taken aback. If a person understood people they would not have said they had a mental age of ten, because saying that an adult has a mental age of ten is a derogatory way to describe someone. What Maurice said helped me to realise certain things.

In the stunned silence that had followed what I said to Buck Jones, I went on to add, 'I'm supposed to be autistic.'

Buck Jones, now sitting and talking to me had said, 'Autistic is a term doctors invented to describe children who were backwards.' He went on to describe psychiatrists as being 'full of shit' – is actually what he said.

I would later consider the implications and effects of telling people that I was autistic; if I had known the implications of what I had said, I could have logically analysed it. I also told Buck Jones that I took back what I said about having a mental age of ten and told him that I had not meant it.

'I know you didn't, Bill,' Buck assured me.

Buck, like many people, knew or realised many things that I did not at the time. A person with a mental age of ten might display certain traits and seem different generally speaking than I did. I had two 'O' levels, which was more than around fifty percent of the population; Mark Hawk said I was intelligent and so did a lot of other people, including Maurice Bridgeland.

What I had said to Buck Jones was quite outrageous and bizarre. Mark Hawk told me about people he'd known whose behaviour could be considered very strange; he mentioned a man who could only relieve his angry feelings by running into a church naked and screaming. If I repeated what I said to either Buck Jones or Mark Hawk, I could have made the comparison between these two examples of bizarre behaviour, mine – expressed verbally, and the man Mark mentioned – expressed physically.

When I recalled what I had said to Buck, Mark Hawk just said, 'No,' in his distant way, without even looking at me. AAWV would have asked him why he was saying, 'No,' if what I had said was bizarre. Why? AAWV would have also raised the question of whether the people he knew behaved oddly by running into churches naked, were actually aware that their behaviour was odd.

During a shift with Mark Hawk, I once stretched my upper

body, in an exaggerated move. I had been tired and made a muscle flexing gesture, holding my fists up in the air as part of a physical yawn. Mark Hawk had asked, 'What's that?' I was a little startled. I told him that I was just stretching. I might have done it as example of odd behaviour, to rival or follow the odd behaviour that he had described, but I had not realised I was doing it at the time. I knew I was making a physical movement but was not conscious of how it looked to other people. I could have made it look less odd, by yawning and putting my hand to my mouth when stretching. I could have also discussed with Mark the issue of whether a person was aware of when their behaviour seemed unusual or not to other people. This was a factor that modified people's behaviour that was learnt from an early stage in development. I had begun to develop later than others and would continue to develop at a much slower pace.

Mark talked about another person he knew who had behaved bizarrely, a girl who had wanted to sit on the front of a car, inserting the hood ornament up her vagina. This woman was obviously aware that her behaviour would be considered odd by others, as wanting to sit on the front of a car, inserting the hood ornament up your vagina was the sort of thing a girl would only say they wanted to do consciously, for effect or to shock.

The only significant thing about what the girl did was what Mark had said, 'It must have hurt like hell, since the ornament was sticking into her genitals.' This comment showed that Mark knew more about the female anatomy than I did. He must have learnt it from someone or something, like a book about female sexual organs being as vulnerable to pain as male sexual organs were; it showed that Mark knew more about the world in general than I did. That is something I might have told him but didn't, because I didn't know how he would react.

Mark would frequently say that I lacked confidence. I asked him why he thought I lacked confidence and he said it was because of how I acted and behaved and my general mannerisms. When I asked why he thought I was not confident, what I had meant was the actual reason or reasons why I was not confident, the cause of the condition rather than the symptoms. The reason I was not confident, I would realise later, was because I had not consciously experienced life. I had not consciously had any experiences or done things; it was partly through being MDDB that I had not been able to do anything at all. I had experienced frequent feelings of stimulus through everyday interaction. I had felt like doing things that I did not know but had not. I had not had the confidence to face the fact that I was not confident. I had not been able to do things that might make me more confident. That was another one of the things I could have shared with Mark, but did not.

Mentally, deaf, dumb and blind may have been caused by an inability to process and 'be aware', as my father might say. I probably tried to process too much too fast, or tried to process information in the wrong order. I should have been able to take in a lot of the smaller, mundane things that are taken for granted, such as roads, streets, houses, shops, churches, Portsmouth etc. This would have helped me to understand society in general through understanding Portsmouth and its structure.

Mark Hawk had said his main preoccupation, or one of the things he considered most important was being independent. He had given me a lecture on it one shift, about how our parents would not be around forever. I, myself, had been nagged by my father about my lack of independence. He had told me about it at one time when we had come home from a holiday.

He had been sitting in the dining room and had been looking very glum. When I had asked him why he looked so serious and despondent, he said he was worried. I asked him what about, and he said it was because of what he thought might eventually become of me. He then said I was not independent. I was around fifteen at the time; my father would complain to me on a number of occasions about my lack of independence, right up to and including when I was sixteen. I understood vaguely but did not know how to achieve this. My father had told me it was by doings things. I had told my father I wanted to do things but could not.

'Well, make up your mind you're going to do something, then just do it!' he had once bellowed at me.

I had always stayed in at home, never going out and mingling, making friends. I had no friends to go out with or meet because I could not get out in the first place. I had seen Maurice once when I was nineteen and asked how I could be more mature. At the time, I was becoming more aware of my own social contact with others and how it affected me. There was a time when I had faced up to the fact that I was not confident. That may have been only a temporary breakthrough in facing up to my problems and needs.

Maurice had told me the very fact that I had asked him about becoming mature was interesting. He probably saw it as a sign of social progression. Maurice had suggested I could become more mature by being independent. He had ended the meeting by suggesting I start doing things rather than talking and thinking about doing things. The things he had suggested were things like tidying up my room and even cleaning it, and changing my clothes without being told.

Mark Hawk had also talked about doing things in order to be independent. He had told me if I felt like doing something to just do it. At the time I had not been able to do anything at all. I could have posed to him the fact that I thought becoming more confident was just as, if not more, important than becoming more independent, or overcoming my fear of the dark. Lack of confidence, I could have told him, would hold me back just as much as being afraid of the dark, or lack of independence.

The job was getting to be too much. I was feeling relatively less mentally deaf, dumb and blind but was still very switched off. It seemed I never had time to view the situation from a distance. All the hours I had to work seemed to be making me more confused. I had complained to Dave the supervisor and to Nigel, a higher supervisor. Mark had overheard me discussing it and said that he planned how he was going to spend his free time. Free time existed outside the sixty to seventy-two hours that made up the time spent on the job.

I had argued with the higher supervisor, Nigel, about the hours and he eventually told me that if I didn't like them, I could resign. In my switched off state, I was aware of time going past, but while I was on Fraser Battery's gatehouse for hours, doing nothing, I felt it was all going past without me being aware of it. If I had been in a job where I was required to do more, like being on days at Fraser Battery, and was able to do it, it might have helped me to concentrate. Concentrating might have helped me to be able to understand the job in sequence. I would be more able to understand the things in the job one at a time, rather than all at once.

Hefin Thomas, the General Manager, had come down to Fraser Battery on a visit, to check our efficiency. We had discussed whether I wanted to stay on, if I did, he wanted to see an improvement in my mental alertness. Then and there, that night I had filled in a form telling him I had resigned. He seemed relieved that I had finally made a decision about it.

Chapter 15

Moving On

I was relieved I had resigned from Fraser Battery; I had experienced a lot of stress caused by the burden of the long hours and the confusion they caused. I would experience appalling frustration that would rise up and just explode. I would shout and scream at passers-by, and anything else. The anger was not just focused, it was a tantrum. I would not swear – swearing was something I still could not do. The frustration would occur without cause, such as when I was out patrolling Fraser Battery; I had once smashed the clock I was carrying against a wall. Another stressful situation occurred when I was wheeling my bike down to Fraser's one day.

I was still upset over the incident with the girls. It was anger, a feeling for vengeance. One time I was at home when I had got uptight and had brought a stool down on the floor of the dining room; my family had been gathered round me. My mother had been quite sympathetic, but twice my father and brother had been frustrated. I had told my family about what had happened with the girls and my brother said he thought it might have been the uniform that caused the attack.

'I bet they call the police pigs,' stated my brother. He meant the fact that policemen wore uniforms as well.

I still occasionally saw one of the girls round Cosham. When she saw me she would abuse me, usually with just one word, 'Wanker'. AAWV would have later thought of saying, 'Thinking about you would cure that, love!'

Once I left a bicycle pump in a bank, coming out the girl had passed me with a friend walking beside her. 'Watch out!' I heard her say, 'He's a real Din. Weirdo!'

AAWV would have later thought of saying, 'Did you say Dinlow? I've got two 'O' levels, love, in English and History. That's about what forty per cent of the population have. As for being weird, that's something I'm working on changing.'

Around the time I had slammed the chair down in the dining room, I had confessed to my mother that I was scared of the girl. My mother was taken aback a bit, as was my brother.

'Why, she's only a woman?' my mother had said, rather exasperatedly.

'She's only a woman.' My brother had said the same thing, 'Less than that.'

Social cognitive would later realise the stigma and absurdity for some men, of being afraid of someone who, like a woman, was physically weaker than them. I still could not empathise with others enough to recognise and understand their individual characteristics. Often I took their characteristics at face value and not recognise the person underneath, that had been the reason for my nervousness of the girl. I knew she was fearsome but that was all I knew about her.

If someone wanted to scare and dominate me they could, but they could no longer order me around as much as they once could. If someone had told me to stand on a particular spot, I would consider and think about what they said, and not necessarily obey it.

Six months after I had finished the security job, I enrolled with the Portsmouth Training Agency, PETA (Portsmouth Engineering Training Agency). The introduction consisted of the usual introductions to a scheme, and to each other. The DHSS had obliged me to go on the scheme; failure to comply would mean loss of benefits.

We were introduced to the scheme in a conference room in the civic offices, again. The people who introduced us were the usual cheerful people who mentioned to myself and the group in general, about having a 'positive attitude'. They wrote it on the board facing us. We passed the time with cups of coffee, and games, and aptitude tests.

There was one aptitude test in which I remember scoring quite high – it was a basic Maths and English test. We spent an afternoon on it but at the end, I forgot to put my name on it. I remember thinking that it was a silly thing to do, as now they would not know who had done quite well in both tests. When I mentioned it to one of the supervisors he agreed with me. It was this one particular flaw in what I did, one small mistake that had made, or almost made, everything else I did meaningless.

It has always been, and still is, very important that I am aware of, and understand, the things about my own immediate situation. I should understand it in terms of size and significance, as well as sequence. Understanding things in sequence would be important to me later on in job situations and elsewhere, as part of making mental connections; I would later make connections about sound situations and practical situations. I would also understand sequences of incidents in social situations; what was said and done, what was not said and done in terms of cause and effect, and, how one thing led to another.

I told the people organising the scheme I had a problem with my behaviour. I did not understand it very well beyond what I had been told, but I told them I had difficulty dealing with people. One organiser mentioned that I was smiling to myself when he first met me, he said he remembered wondering what I was smiling at. It was embarrassing for me then, but generally less embarrassing than what had gone before. The same organiser told me I had seemed very intelligent when we first started talking. He asked me what sort of job I wanted and I told him a job in office work, or selling.

'You mean a job which requires some intelligence?' he replied.

'Yes,' I said.

The introduction continued for another few days; we came in and drank coffee in-between lectures. The 'positive attitude' they had talked about was not as easy to apply to my thinking. I had become cynical and despondent over the time I was switched off. I was more switched on now, but the cost had been to make me emotionally weary. I felt I had been in a battle made up of regret and failure; a battle between two worlds and two extremes.

I was eventually offered a place with a pottery company in Denmead; Denmead Potteries was located in the village of that name, over Cosham Hill. I told Denmead Potteries of my difficulty concentrating.

I had not once used the word autism, I never mentioned it to anyone in this sort of situation because it did not occur to me to. At the rehabilitation centre I could, and should, have mentioned it if I had fully known about it. There were not many placements for people with my specific,, and yet vaguely definable, disability. There were not many jobs and placements anyway in Portsmouth.

While there were many who did not realise my disability, I found it hard to identify. It was not like having a limb missing or malfunctioning, as my father had once said. In my case, it was part of my mental make-up that was socially retarded, or socially malfunctioning.

The positions available at Denmead Potteries consisted of either a general worker, or a groundsman for the outdoor area. The groundsman, I now realised, would be needed for things like cutting grass when it became too long. I was told by the scheme supervisors, and later people working at Denmead Potteries, that the job of groundsman would require someone with greater powers of concentration than me; that is why I was not suited to it.

If I had realised certain things about the job, I would have asked or enquired about them, for example why I needed to concentrate on things like the grass growing, and when it would need to be cut, and whether weeding would be required. The job was a long way from Cosham, it was over the hill and around three miles further on and required either going by car or by bike.

I was warned about the distance by the scheme supervisor and by the man in charge at Denmead, Ernie. At the time, I was prepared to take anything without making decisions. I lacked initiative to the point of choosing what happened to me and what I did. There had been a time in the social worker's office at Hilsea when she had mentioned that I had been coming to work everyday on time, but according to her, had not been doing any work. That was one of the few things that I had been aware of.

The job had begun in February; my father had taken me by car to Denmead Potteries. We got lost round the winding roads and arrived ten minutes late. Ernie, a very small middle-aged supervisor had angrily remarked on this, even though I had expected sympathy at getting lost in the countryside around Denmead. I was set on the very simple forms of work such as filling the inside of jugs with paste, and working on the conveyor belt.

My first attempt at filling the jugs had bad results. I had been shown how to do it by pouring paste from a plastic jug into the clay jugs, swilling it round and pouring it back into the container, but had not taken it all in. Ernie had called me back to where the pouring took place, at the back of the building that formed the pottery. He had shown me the jugs and the paste that was all over them.

'You've got to be careful,' he told me. 'You've got paste all over your fingers and everywhere.' Ernie had not told me that I had to be careful not to get paste on the jugs, or anywhere else.

The jugs were filled with paste then emptied, to coat the insides of them. I had not realised before being shown, or before I arrived at the job, or before I even agreed to the placement, or went to the introduction that I was meant to pay attention to either what happened or what I was shown. I had not told myself I had to pay attention to details of what I saw and was told.

I was not yet fully aware of all the responsibilities of the work situation. If I had been aware of all the responsibilities, I would have realised the importance of paying attention. I would have realised the importance of being more motivated and concentrating more on what I was doing. A job might seem easy, but it always seemed as though there was something I was not doing, that I had overlooked or something that I was not doing properly.

Chapter 16

Revelation and Frustration

*U*p until I started at Denmead, I would still feel angry at the way I had been treated by the girls at the railway bridge. The anger was now reduced to being focused on the one fat girl I occasionally saw round Cosham. There was an occasion I was feeling angry and upset, it was in the night and I found I had to get up to go to the toilet. It was one of many occasions that I felt like getting up and going to the toilet.

I was sitting in our toilet with the light on and was still feeling upset at the thought of all the savage spite I had been subjected to. I felt scared and upset, like I had been with the students at college, and Mark Burns before. I sat brooding about my own feelings; my anger at being angry and my fear of being afraid.

Then I had this feeling of where I was. Where was I? I was sitting on the toilet in the bathroom. I had a feeling of purely logical thought. Was the girl here, near me? No. Then what was I upset about? The feeling struck me and gripped me as though everything else was insignificant. I felt more mature; I felt more mature because something told me I was more mature. It was as though all my thoughts had become focused in one place and at one time. All my thoughts were focused on reality and realistic thinking; I had a moment of realisation. It was something I found could only come from my efforts, it was a process of effort equalling accumulation.

I later read a book by Stephen King called *It*; the book dealt at some point with a boy sitting in a classroom worrying about having to deal with a bully after school. The boy experiences the same self-realisation that I did, together with all the accompanying feelings. The feeling comes to the boy, not through what he feels but through what he thinks. The extract mentions him becoming aware of his first logical cold-blooded thought. I had felt myself think, not about fantasy but about what I was actually doing, feeling, touching, walking. I imagined my relations with others, I myself, listening to them, and judging when to talk and not to talk – I could judge when to listen and when to avoid interrupting others.

Later, when I was downstairs in the kitchen, I pondered over what had happened to me, I wondered where it would lead me. I felt I could do anything, and I actually felt like doing things – it was me that had made myself feel what I had felt; it was exciting what I was feeling, but it was also frightening. The boy in the Stephen King book had found it disturbing; he was around ten, I was now twenty-two.

The feeling had come about while I was thinking about someone who had scared me to the point of shock. It was as though they had broken through a barrier, separating me from the outside world. Fear and hardship may have caused me to think about the world around me, and caused me to respond. The boy in the book, it was said, now faced no way back from mental and emotional adulthood; I could identify with that. It also said that as he grew up, he would think more in that same way. I found then, as now, that the feeling came – if I made it come. I knew if I kept to it and constantly practised it, it would eventually change my whole life, but I could not commit myself indefinitely. I would feel it, but then would put it off.

I later felt that I had experienced something akin to a religious experience. It had been so simple and yet so blinding. I felt it had temporarily changed me; I wondered if other people found that kind of feeling came more naturally to them, and whether they needed to be consciously aware of it. Was it something that comes to them a lot younger, like the boy in the book? Did it have to come through a tumultuous or stressed experience, like myself and the boy in the book? Does the condition of autism run counter to the experience I had had or is the condition of autism itself part of the absence of the experience I had had, and an inability to feel it?

While I was feeling it, I found it impossible to have tantrums, but I still did have tantrums when I started work. They would mainly occur when I got lost on the way home from work, or when I was late to work or it was raining. The tantrums were totally uncontrolled and hysterical; they were hysterical in the sense that I could not control them, they became something I could not control or think about.

The experience I had may have been the very early forerunner to AAWV and socially cognitive, or may have been added to them. It was set alongside extremely angry and emotive feelings that were incredibly frustrated. The anger and frustration may have been the result of years of suppressed motivation and energy, and the inability to achieve things in everyday life.

Coinciding with this revelation, I began to experience what may have been irritable bowel syndrome. I would lie in bed at night and would experience a feeling down below of wanting to go to the toilet but found when sitting on it, I could not go. I would go back to bed, then the feeling would come back. The feeling was of there being something in my lower intestine that had to come out but could not.

I would go back to the toilet and try to relieve myself, again there would be no result. This would go on and on, and I would get so frustrated I would shout and scream or stomp my feet on the floor, which caused a lot of frustration and anxiety for my parents, but at the time I felt I could not help it. At night, I would be lying in bed wanting to sleep, to enjoy beautiful rest but could not. Looking back, I wonder if it may have been partly suppressed energy that meant sleep was not all that important. The times it happened, I did not get seriously tired, not to the extent of finding myself dozing off; I would doze off eventually however while in bed. I harboured a latent fear that I might mess the bed in the same way a person might wet it. I would later find that if I relaxed my stomach muscles and became less tense, it helped the feeling to go away. It also helped later if I ignored the feeling completely and pretended it did not exist.

A few days later my mother told me how I had woken up our neighbour in her bed; our bathroom had a large window facing the neighbour's house. I had been sitting in the bathroom; I was tired; I had been thinking about things people had said to me in the past, all the banal frustrating things. It was dark when I screamed, I was not scared, I just screamed and shouted.

The neighbour was a friend of ours; she was also a child psychologist, which made her more understanding. The complaint however was very embarrassing for me, as no problem, however extreme, could justify my behaviour. The actions I had taken and the violent emotions I had expressed could be compared with psychosis schizophrenia, and sometimes depression in terms of how it manifested itself; that is what a psychiatrist or psychologist might say. Autism is sometimes viewed as a mental illness and could be categorised as being like the aforementioned illnesses in terms of manifestation and symptom; to others it could have come across just as a tantrum.

When I told Maurice that my main job at the Pottery was working on a conveyor belt he commented that I had a good brain, insinuating or stating that I deserved a more demanding job than working on something repetitive. I had worked in another job at the pottery, rubbing bits of pottery to wear them down and then blowing them with air to blow away the dust. I kept losing the stone I had to use to rub them with and had to retrieve it from the machine. I occasionally asked about other jobs I could do. Ernie would respond with a wry smile and say that someone else did those jobs. What he meant to say was that he did not trust me with jobs that were more complex than the conveyor belt job.

One job that was mentioned was sorting out different products such as plates, animal shapes and saucers. I realised later that I could have done that particular job if it was as simple as the small jobs I had done in-between the conveyor belt job. These small jobs were very similar to the other job, in that they involved sorting out potteries from different crates; later I would be more aware of how potteries, like factories and many other places of work were organised, and what jobs were connected with them. Possibly, there were jobs that required speed as well as accuracy at the pottery. I had been put on the rubbing and blowing job for a certain amount of time then taken off. I was told it was because I was too slow.

At lunchtime, this was mentioned among workmates and the lad who normally did the job, aged sixteen, joked that there must be a 'Knack to it'. It may have seemed strange to think about a person learning to work faster, but when the lad had mentioned this, and after I had been taken off the job, I realised the need to work faster. I tried working faster whenever I was doing rubbing and blowing but still kept making mistakes.

I went through a period when I started being more motivated and started working harder and faster. Ernie had been pleased but rather amused and had told me to slow down. I would work the conveyor belt faster, sort out crates and what was in them faster. I would rub and blow faster but was still not properly focused, and still not as mentally agile as I needed to be. I was occasionally told I was slow on the conveyor belt as well. My job on that was to take products off and put them on another conveyor belt that worked on wheels. If they were chipped or scraped I had to paint over bits of them. I had to wipe them on a wet cloth and if I scraped off too much I had to paint over those bits.

Ernie once said to me, 'I don't know how you can have a full line.' Meaning when the conveyor belt was full up with products. He also said that the trouble with me was that I did not move, he said this as he was taking over the conveyor belt while I was doing something else, he started unloading the plates and mugs and ornaments faster than I did. The other problem the scheme had with me was a tendency of mine to go to the toilet and spend time there; it was an extension of the problem I had at home. I would feel like going to the toilet the same way I did at home when I was in bed, during the night. I would want to spend a few minutes in the toilet but would spend eight, or sometimes ten minutes in there; it was the feeling of stomach tension that would cause it.

Ernie had once commented on it, telling me I had spent ten minutes in the toilet, as he stood, confronting me as I emerged. One other lad complained to me about it and banged on the door to make the point.

'You building a toilet in there rather than using one?' he

commented, as I emerged to let him in. The situation became so bad that my case worker on PETA wanted to discuss it when I met him. He read from a report on me, 'You've been spending a lot of time in the toilet'. I did not at the time realise the practical implications of my behaviour in a social context, however, I realised the implications to a greater degree in employment terms, in that the time spent in the toilet, was time spent distracted and away from work.

Ernie could not be around all the time, which gave me the excuse to indulge my problem. I was growing more confident and experienced of work situations – I was more aware of what I could get away with as an employee. The social aspect was not as clearly defined to me, and as usual I did not realise how my behaviour would be interpreted by others, in this case being interpreted as odd. Practical cognitive was more understanding than social cognitive.

I was still very quiet but not in the mentally-fear-mute state that I had been in previously. The other workers were a mixed bunch, many younger than me and many women. The women would sit at one end of the room we used to spend lunchtimes and break-times in; the blokes would sit at the other end. In between chatting one lunchtime, the women started laughing hysterically to each other. After a few minutes, one bloke nudged me and suggested they were taking the piss out of me. They seemed to be generally laughing in my direction and the lad, a seventeen year-old, suggested I do it back to them.

'These women, they're the weaker sex,' he urged me. This was a social belief that I was gradually understanding, the humiliation that a man might feel at being dominated by a woman. The belief was also related to the practical fact that women were weaker than men, a fact that influenced male perceptions.

The lad, Dave, or 'Twiggy' as he had been called because of his thin frame, had suggested I take the piss out of them at the same time the following lunchtime.

The following day at lunchtime I did not start laughing, or teasing the women. When the time came, Dave reminded me but I did not start, I did not know how to be 'funny' with the women or how to tease them. The teasing, if any had been intended, had not bothered me much anyway; I should have told Dave this. I could have also told Dave that later on, I discovered they had been laughing because my fly had been undone. The women had not told me directly because they were too embarrassed.

The only woman who still bothered me was the one who had tormented me in Cosham and who occasionally still saw me. I would get angry about her, and the anger was taken out one lunchtime on the chairs in the lunch-room – I had been throwing them around but when Dave heard this, he thought it was because of the women workers at Denmead. He continued to encourage me to give them stick back.

'Don't hit them,' he said, as a piece of worldly advice. 'Don't be afraid of them,' as another piece of worldly advice. He then gave me an example of the sort of foul-mouthed abuse he said I should give the women. I disliked hearing it, and was generally unfamiliar with it.

There was one woman I was warned about from the outset by the other women at work; I found out about her in due course, she was a middle-aged, normal looking woman. She was also a workplace bully. Her patronising, pleasant manner was how she intervened with what you were doing, as well as lecturing you about it. I tried ignoring her when she tried telling me how to do a job such as filling a pot.

The youngest lad at the pottery, a sixteen-year-old who

normally did the rubbing and blowing, told me he just told her to piss off when she had tried to order him around. He added that he was younger than I was.

Does greater maturity get reflected in greater assertiveness? This was part of an issue concerning maturity that had been in my mind, or rather at the back of it for a long time. I was physically twenty-two, I would feel perfectly emotionally mature on some levels and in some situations, and emotionally immature in others. I had 'grown up' viewing maturity from the point of view of my own consciousness and my own experience.

I had told the woman at work to piss off a few times. She had said, 'What?' as a challenge to what I said, as we stood at a workbench over some pottery products. I was used to abuse from people but not so much to being generally ordered around. At the time I could not be assertive, AAWV had not fully emerged. I could not think of the appropriate words to use; MDDB prevented me thinking about the situation.

'I'm only trying to show you how to do a particular task,' the woman would wail.

'You're not a supervisor, you don't have any rank, so I'm not taking anything from you. I don't have to take orders or advice from you.' This was what social or practical cognitive would have told me to say, but it would have also depended on how I said it, as much as what I said. A firm tone would have been needed, which would rely on other things such as greater social and emotional focus.

Dave once asked me if I was alright one morning. At first I thought he meant it as a greeting as in, 'Alright mate'. Later, I began to realise it may have been him enquiring as to whether I was 'normal', as he may have begun to notice some things that were odd about me. It was just outside the lunch and break-time room. If I had interpreted what he said then and there, in the way I had later, I would not have really known what to say. I may have felt uneasy about discussing my disability if I was unaware of it.

My disability was apparent to some people anyway through my general body language; my odd movements and the odd way I usually expressed myself. I felt wary about mentioning or discussing my disability with certain types of people. These were people I thought may be less knowledgeable and less tolerant than others; this may not have been totally unjustified however. It cannot be denied that the less well-educated a person might be, the greater the chances are of them being more prejudiced.

There was a new bloke who was with us briefly, he may have been part-time or temporary. He looked older than his nineteen or twenty years because he wore a moustache. He was tall, broad and fat. He had been in the lunchtime room and was sitting talking with Dave. He had made some remarks in my direction that were rather insulting, or could have been considered rather insulting on the surface.

Remarks about me wandering into the toilets and flashing in public were really part and parcel of the route the piss-taking took; they did not hurt or offend me at the time. The remarks themselves were what I was used to, it was as if the remarks were bouncing off me. If they were not getting through it was because I was not letting them get through completely, in the same way I had not allowed them to get through in the past.

I was unaffected by the new bloke's remarks at first but they became fiercer, not in terms of what was said but in terms of how it was said. He and Dave began to sound more contemptuous in their tone, and boisterous; I sensed there was something different. Lunchtime ended and they left – I began to feel fed up and frustrated as I returned to work.

After an hour working the conveyor belt, the supervisor, a bloke slightly older than Dave and more affable, told me he wanted me to go out into the backyard of the pottery and dump some surplus dried clay; it was full of just that, or products that had got broken. By this time I was very angry and frustrated, and upset. I dragged the bag of surplus dried clay outside to dump it in the large metal skip; it was full of rubbish as I emptied the bag in.

I always got picked on I thought, it was so frustrating and upsetting; I could not deal with it, I had never been able to deal with people's behaviour towards me. Whatever the social situation, I always felt upset by the way people spoke to me, and about me, whether it was to my face or behind my back. I never knew whether to hit someone if they teased me or not. It was all because I had a problem; I had had it my whole life. I felt distracted because my feelings had again dominated my thoughts, rather than the other way around. My lack of actual thought, whether social cognitive or practical cognitive, was preventing me from analysing the reasons for my feelings, or it was blocking out bad feelings completely.

All the time this was going on in my head, I had been wandering around the yard feeling miserable, and sorry for myself, and sulking. I realised I had spent far more time than I needed to dump the rubbish but had not cared. I had started going back to the building when the supervisor appeared and told me that he was going to send out a 'search party' for me because I had been out so long. I told him I had something on my mind and went back to work.

Later, I saw one of the girls who had been in the lunchtime room talking to the supervisor. The supervisor turned to me and said, 'Someone been picking on you? Those two lads?'

Those two lads were Dave and the new bloke. The usual group of women had been in the lunchtime room and noticed the way the men had been talking to me, and had told the supervisor. The supervisor told me that he now understood why I had got upset, and strayed away when I was out in the backyard. I was grateful for the women's support. The two bullies, or possibly would-be bullies, had been hauled up before Ernie and given a good telling off. Ernie had told me I was not in the job to be bullied, and if anyone was to have a go at me for being slow or careless it was him.

When the two lads saw me again they denied they had been picking on me.

'We weren't picking on you,' they told me. They may have been, I later realised, just winding me up. Dave had wound me up before at certain times, like at lunchtime the same day the more serious incident had occurred. The way he had done it was more subtle and had not got to me much; it was just general horseplay on his part. He had done things like imitate the way he thought I ate, making grunting noises as I ate my sandwiches.

There was one woman at Denmead Potteries who seemed quite quiet and stolid, and whom I might have quite liked, but she did not seem to like me too much; she thought I was stupid. We once had a problem with one of the machines and were bouncing it up and down to try to get it started. It was the machine I was supposed to be in charge of and the woman had said something like, 'Bill, even you can't be that stupid!' I knew I was not stupid, or was not supposed to be, but maybe I was stupid in practical terms. That was the impression I could give to people like the woman.

Maurice Bridgeland had constantly told me that social experiences like those encountered on the course were good for my social development, and thus good for helping my problem – the problem he had told me about.

Chapter 17

A Sense of Self

*I*t was in the middle of the year that I had begun searching for something to occupy my spare time, which was as usual, with the advice and encouragement of my mother. She had made suggestions about things I could join and get involved in. My mother had been encouraging me this way since I was aged about fourteen or fifteen. My father had been frustrated that I could not be more self motivated enough to do things for myself. He had told me I did not seek out the experience of life; it was part of the lecture he gave me about my lack of independence.

I realised I knew what he meant when he said seeking out experience but had not been able to do it. I had tried joining an archery club; when I failed to contact the organiser by phone, I had screamed, 'I don't want to be anything!' I had been in the downstairs corridor standing beside the phone. It was an expression of my feeling that if I could not do anything like finding out about a club, getting the phone number and generally organise joining a club, I did not want to be anything. This action was the only way I could express and release anger and it had a funny effect on my brother. He mentioned a French philosopher who came to the conclusion that he could not prove he existed; it was a melodramatic statement.

The archery club lasted one lesson before I gave it up. I

could not discipline myself to keep to something the way I had tried to do with my kung fu.

My brother and mother had been distraught at this. My mother later suggested, how about something like a public speaking course. This was the first step in something that would change my entire life. I went through a list of organisations in the directory in the central library to find one; a public speaking course was held at Priory School in the middle of Portsmouth, just before Southsea.

The course was a series of lessons held at 7.30 pm on Mondays. It was held in an outdoor building, facing the main building of the school. The inside consisted of a set of chairs and tables which we, the class, could seat ourselves in. The man who was taking us was Bill Thompson, a curly-haired, early middle-aged man who wore glasses, and who on our first night, greeted us to the course by allowing us to say our names, and what we wanted to get from the course. Many of us had put down that we wanted to become more confident. This included me.

Bill Thompson also invited us to say what we had wanted to do when we were children. I think I put down that I had wanted to join the army. Bill Thompson, when the list came to him, had said that he had wanted to be a professional footballer when he was a child.

Bill Thompson had started the lesson by saying that lack of confidence was due to lack of preparation. I had not understood this, and posed the question to him of how a person can become more confident if they are not born confident, and thus, cannot prepare. (At the time I was locked in my MDDB world of incomprehension.) I was later to realise that by lack of preparation, Bill Thompson meant lack of experiences, or lack of achievement. When I mentioned this to Maurice Bridgeland, about lack of preparation causing lack of confidence, he agreed by saying that it was because I had not been successful at anything, like an interest or a job or a relationship.

Bill Thompson seemed so intelligent to me, and possibly to the rest of the group, that I had talked to him as often as possible. This was because I enjoyed talking to intelligent people, because I was intelligent myself and because I felt he could supply answers to some of the many questions I had. I told him I had some sort of problem as we walked back to his house from Priory School; the class had ended and I was still talking to him

'What problem?' he had asked. 'Who told you you had a problem?'

I replied that it was my child psychologist, Maurice Bridgeland. I may have said psychiatrist by mistake, instead of psychologist because Bill Thompson said, 'You actually see a psychiatrist?'

Bill Thompson was dismissive about psychiatrists, thinking they encouraged the idea of madness rather than curing madness itself.

Bill saw psychologists as just stupid, and later on referred to Maurice Bridgeland as 'a twit'. Bill Thompson thought madness, or what was considered madness, could be cured by social interaction, by which he meant social stimulus. When I told Maurice Bridgeland that he believed in social interaction to treat madness, Maurice was illuminated.

'That's wonderful,' he said over the phone.

'What do you mean?' I replied.

'Well ask him to show you the social directions.' When I had said social interaction to Maurice, he had thought Bill Thompson had meant social understanding and that

Bill Thompson thought he could help me with it – social understanding could stem from social interaction as it became both a product of and a requirement for social interaction.

I walked home with Bill Thompson every Monday evening and often continued speaking to him in his home. I told him about the problem I was supposed to have, not knowing how other people work and asked him if he had any advice. All he could offer was,'The establishment of a moral level of behaviour when meeting another person. For example,' he continued, 'if you were to start hitting them with a hammer, having knocked them to the ground, it would not only be contrary to their interests but would be liable legally.'

The example he had just stated, was an extreme version of how social behaviour affects another person. What we could have discussed was a more subtle aspect of social situations. He said social situations boiled down to whether a person who did that had affected another person's interests. I had asked him if he minded me picking my nose, and he said no but he did mind me wiping it on the furniture of his study.

I still ate sweets. I once asked Bill Thompson if he minded me opening a bag of sweets during the lessons; Bill said he did not mind. What he did mind was whether or not I handed them round to other members of the group; Bill thought I had a moral obligation to do so; Bill Thompson hated selfishness.

I had occasionally told him about the feelings I had had at the beginning of the year, and how I had come to realise these as a 'sense of self'. The 'sense of self' tended to irritate Bill when I used these words to describe what was really a social or mental consciousness.

'You're talking about being aware of yourself.' Whenever I mentioned 'self awareness', he would retort, 'Why not be aware of other people?' These two statements along with, 'thinking about myself', as I occasionally said, were misinterpreted by Bill. These feelings were in fact, the beginning of social and practical cognitive, and were seen as selfish by Bill Thompson.

I wonder how he would have reacted if I had told him the feelings of self were, to put it differently, part of the mind coming to terms with its possessor and the world around it.

Bill Thompson had told me that in terms of social behaviour, there was no absolute social standard for every situation. Bill cited the way a person in one situation behaved, such as someone in a nightclub, was different from the way a person in another situation, such as in church, might be expected to behave. Bill went on to cite cultural differences in behaviour such as an Eskimo sharing his wife with another person, and an Englishman not being prepared to do likewise.

It occurred to me later that the differences in social behaviour would need, to a certain extent, to be navigated by the person concerned. Social navigation could be achieved by being aware of the social situation, for example, being aware of what was done in a nightclub was not done in a church.

I had introduced myself to a woman who lived at Bill's house. Bill had commented that I claimed to have a problem understanding how to relate to people, yet had introduced myself to the woman he lived with.

The time came, when after reciting to Bill all the experiences I had had, which made me feel odd when I remembered them, I told him how I had told the man I worked with at Reliance Security that I had a mental age of ten. Bill Thompson had stiffened when he heard this and had looked at me for a long time; we had been walking from Priory School and were just outside his house in the garden. He was just before the door when he heard what I said.

'Why did you say that?' he asked slowly and deliberately.

'I don't know, I just felt like it.' I said it was all I could remember. The effect of what I said had been a lot for even him to understand. He could not comprehend why I had said it. He viewed all behaviour, or at least most behaviour, as having some logical explanation. The reason I had said what I said, was because I had not been aware of the implications of what I said, or the effect it had on others. While not directly affecting or damaging another person's interests, my behaviour could still seem odd to other people. The fact that I had said what I said, might mean in itself that I had some sort of mental illness; this was considering that mental illness was often measured by outrageous behaviour.

Actually I did have a mental illness in having Asperger's Syndrome, if Asperger's Syndrome is an illness. I had been discussing mental illness with Bill Thompson and questioned whether he could judge it. He had stopped and told me, 'Look! I have a relative who has an illness called Asperger's Syndrome,' he paused glaring at me, 'and they are just completely and totally gone.'

How ironic that is now; I had not heard of Asperger's Syndrome until then. Bill Thompson had mentioned it a few times in the lessons; he had been wandering from the subject of public speaking to the subject of mental illness and had cited Asperger's Syndrome as an example of an illness that no doctor had properly diagnosed as to its cause, and whose sufferers were completely 'gone'.

The cause of Asperger's Syndrome has not been diagnosed apart from a possible physical origin concerning a part of the brain. Interestingly, I had had a brain scan that year at Queen Alexandra's hospital. This was because I had shouted and screamed to such a degree one night that I had woken up my father. He had demanded that I take the test. It was more for his peace of mind than anything else. Wires had been glued to my head then switched on; there was no sign of brain abnormality.

The fact that my Asperger's Syndrome is relatively mild is the reason there was no recorded physical abnormality in my brain. The fact that Asperger's Syndrome is itself a mild form of autism, may be the reason it is less well documented as having a physical origin. I read in the autobiography of the Hollywood film star, Sylvester Stallone that he has a son who is autistic. The book states that a brain test was made on the boy; no brain damage or abnormality was recorded for him; it optimistically states that he could conceivably recover.

The irony was that if, as Bill Thompson claimed, 'All those with AS were completely gone' then it would have been impossible for me to talk to him and have a relationship with him. I had also mentioned autism to Bill Thompson; it was something I had heard mentioned at various times in my life in vague reference to me.

'Isn't there some sort of physical reason for it?'

After all the heavy discussion I had with Bill Thompson about a whole lot of social subjects, Bill had once asked me as we were almost at his house, 'Look, what do you want?'

'What do you mean?' I replied.

'I mean, what do you want to do?'

'I don't know,' I said in honesty.

'Well, find out what it is you want to do, then do it.' And with that he walked off home.

Later, on another occasion, we were in his house when he repeated the question.

'What do you want to do, Bill? What do you want to be?' he meant basically what sort of career did I want as the main aim of my life, but he asked rhetorically, 'Why not become a millionaire?' then, 'Why not kill someone?'

All my depression, all the frustration and sulky bitterness I had felt all my life came to the surface.

'I don't want to be anything,' I told Bill Thompson. I had decided it in my mind as revenge on the world around me, on life for all the betrayals, and on myself for being a party to the betrayal. The way Bill responded was the way I thought and anticipated he would respond.

'You'll have to be something, Bill,' he told me. 'You'll have to be.' He meant by 'being', having a job, 'Or eventually you'll starve.'

'I'm lazy,' I told him with a certain amount of self-honesty.

'Well, I'm lazy,' Bill admitted. 'I don't want to do my job,' he said, pointing to a pile of essays from the other students he taught on a table. 'But I have to because if I didn't I'd eventually starve – it's the same for everybody.'

I did not understand at the time about the way I felt. The reason I had felt depressed and upset, and had not been able to do anything, was because of the problem that was holding me back. In the past it had been an inability to concentrate and an inability to think. I had told Bill Thompson that I did not think. He had replied by saying what he himself had often said before, that people did not think. What he meant as a personal belief, was that people did not think on an intellectual level. When I said it about myself, I had meant it on a practical level. I had meant thinking about the immediate everyday things, like crossing a road, or meeting people. My inability to think and concentrate was part of the reason I had not done anything.

'All those people in everyday life, they don't want to do their job but they have to because if they didn't they would starve.' He also said, as I thought he would, that it was rather shameful of me, since all those other people are working and trying to fulfil ambitions.

I left that night after Bill had told me there was a reason I did not want to be anything. Bill was often asking questions about why people said and did things, that was one of the reasons I enjoyed talking to him.

The year was drawing to a close and the course at Denmead Potteries was coming to an end, without any sign of my gaining employment there; I felt I had been drifting through it, as though in some sort of dream. My father had gone in there to speak to the chief supervisor Ernie about me having a job, also that I was too old to be paid the same wage that a sixteen-year-old would be paid. I had seen my father talking to Ernie and I had seen Ernie indicating and pointing to a workbench and realised he was talking about an incident when I had been told to clean the workbench but had forgotten.

'You've done a wonderful job on it mate,' Ernie had stated sarcastically. He was telling my father that I was not reliable and could not concentrate properly; my father had later repeated this to me.

We were in the car driving back from Denmead Potteries. My father had seemed uptight about something, he seemed agitated. I asked him what he wanted. 'I just want you to get a job!' he yelled, hitting the steering wheel in his frustration. Previously, I had told him I had found it exciting deciding what sort of job I wanted, I was feeling reborn as a person as though I was finally beginning to live. He had just grunted at hearing this.

I told him I had been worried.

"Well, I'm worried too, Bill,' he said miserably. By worried, I had meant worried that I did not know what job I wanted and was not into a chosen career yet. My father was worried that I had never worked and may never work.

The job at Denmead had been making me late for every

public speaking lesson. The first time had been embarrassing for me; I had walked in almost thirty minutes into the lesson. Bill Thompson, lecturing the class and teaching them, had responded almost amused. He talked to me in front of the class about the distance from Denmead to Portsmouth before I sat down.

The time came at the end of the Public Speaking course when I saw Bill Thompson about it. Bill asked me if I had been reading the notes he had given me at the beginning of the course. I told him I had not.

'Thirty minutes a week Bill,' Bill Thompson had bellowed in the study of his house. 'Thirty minutes a week on Sunday afternoons.' He was referring to the time he had advised us to spend revising the notes he had given us.

'The examiner is actually going to be sitting at a table in a room. You will sit down and be expected to make a speech, showing your grasp of public speaking and you do your idiot act, for example getting out a bag of sweets,' he continued angrily and exasperated. Then he ended by asking me, 'What exactly have you done over the last ten years, Bill?' What he said struck a chord with me, it was one of the focal points of my life as he said it there in his study.

'Oh, nothing much,' I replied.

'Well, that's ten years gone that can never be regained.'

I had been conscious of time going past but had not been curious of it going past in that way; the memory of time lost had made me afraid of it. I had kept putting off fulfilling impulses, such as having interests and carrying out activities. I had told Bill I had always felt like hitting someone once I was close enough.

'Why don't you?' Bill had asked, in a usually eccentric way. I would have told him I was not brave enough, if it had occurred to me at the time. I had told him about all the anger I felt that came out in my shouting when on my bike, and other tantrums I had had in the street. Bill had brought this up in the discussion we were having on what I had been doing over the last ten years. He told me, 'All your anger isn't from frustration at being late, Bill, it comes from suppressed motivation.'

'If that's the case,' I asked, 'What do you think I should do to accommodate the anger?'

'Work,' he suggested. I knew what he meant; I had anticipated it. By working, Bill meant doing things and making the effort, by this he also meant working on what I wanted to do in terms of a future career, plus achievements in activities and interests. The suggestion that I work made an impression on me over the next few days. It made me think of all I had not done in the last ten years.

Chapter 18

Parting with Daydreams

What Bill Thompson had said made me more active and more motivated to do things. I tried finding out about guitar lessons. A friend at church had asked me if I had considered it as an interest and I was inspired; at the time I was involved in a 'teach and reach' activity at my Christian church.

I had been curious about the Christian faith and also about my own faith, namely because I did not really have any of my own. Some time ago, when I was attending college, a big bearded man had met me at a Christian friend's house and explained the Christian faith to me. One of the things the man brought up was the subject of love – he meant love in the Christian sense. I had only ever understood love in a sexual sense; my autistic condition may have prevented me from feeling and appreciating emotions. I had never really loved someone emotionally, apart from the feelings I once had at the rehabilitation centre for a girl I once found attractive, whom I might have loved.

That night, when I had considered all that I had been told about God and love, I had experienced something. It was not a blinding spiritual experience, it was a feeling of love inside me. It was something that may have been awakened; the ability to love people as the Christian religion teaches. It may have been something of the world that was getting through to me via religion; it was social reactions over a long period, becoming emotions.

When I told my Christian friends I had felt God's love they were overjoyed. What had gone into me socially, had caused me in turn, to return something outwardly – to give. I would talk to some people later about how more seemed to be going out, as part of a greater relationship with the world around me. One Christian man said it was caused by a spiritual quality that had been formed through spiritual experiences.

After I had proclaimed what I thought was my new faith, the bearded man, who had originally explained to me the Christian faith, asked me what I wanted to do as a career. I told him I was studying at college and was on the YTS as a caretaker but had no idea what I wanted to do for a career. Later on, when I met the man again, he asked me if I had a job and I said no, that I had given up my job with the security firm. The man had recommended another security firm I applied to but I was not successful. He had also enquired if I had any interests; I told him I did kung fu, which at the time, I did. He suggested I take up some less violent hobby like playing an instrument like the guitar, which was now what I intended to do for an interest. It was something I hoped might lead to some sort of career.

The next time I had seen Bill Thompson he continued our usual discussion about me doing things and what I needed to do in the future. As we were walking back to his house I told him that I intended to be a professional guitarist.

'Oh really,' he had responded. 'How long have you been practising?'

'I've just begun lessons.'

'How many songs can you play?'

'None at all.'

'Well,' he said, 'that would take a minimum of three years of intense practice to learn and develop, then you'd have to find a sponsor.'

We were almost at his house.

'What is it you really want to do, Bill?'

'I don't know,' I replied.

'You haven't any idea at all?' he enquired.

'No,' I replied. I sensed the reaction I wanted from him; that somehow he could tell me the answer, or one of the answers, to the riddle of my existence and the world around me.

'How old are you?' he asked. I replied what I might have told him before that I was twenty three.

'Then that shows you haven't done anything over the last ten years. As we grow older, Bill, from the time we're around ten or eleven, we develop in terms of future career plans. We find out what we're good at; I wanted to be a football player but I developed a knee injury, as a result I had to give it up and move on to something else – an academic career.' He was pausing in front of his house door. I knew what was to come might be terrible, but I still wanted to know it.

'It's unfortunate, very unfortunate that you don't know what you want to do at twenty three because most people, by the time they're eighteen, have at least a vague idea of what they want to do for a living. You'll have to work five times harder than other people Bill, you'll have to make a lot of difficult decisions and make a lot of compromises.' He looked at me tragically, then slowly said. 'I wouldn't want to be in your shoes for anything, Kiddo. Not,' he paused, 'for anything.'

I was shocked. I knew it was leading to something terrible but real; the culmination of drifting for ten years had led to a revelation. The ten, or even more, years that had built up had come to a head; maybe I was lucky to have met Bill Thompson at that age.

I had a voice in my head that had started speaking as Bill had entered his house, and I had started for home. I now knew worry; I was worried in a way I had never been worried before. I rode home; I felt more depressed than I had ever felt before. I now seemed oblivious to everything around me, as though ten years had come crashing down on me. I was oblivious, yet I was now becoming more aware of what I did in sequence as I cycled home. I now felt frenzied in my desire to work and to achieve things; I now had ten years' work to fit into the future somehow. I also felt ashamed, because if I did have a problem or disability then I should have been working harder to overcome it. I could not even cry; crying would not help, it would not do anything to change things.

I remembered a Chinese saying I had once heard. 'When you feel the tiger's breath on your neck, it is better to think it is the summer's breeze'. I had the tiger's breath on my neck yet wanted to believe it was just that, and not a summer's breeze. I wanted to face up to my problems squarely and use the feelings they produced, the shock, the near traumatisation combined with greater motivation. If I did not start now I thought, to make up for the lost time of ten years, where would I be in ten years from now?

When I got home, my family noticed how I seemed; I had difficulty eating and sleeping. Eating and sleeping, I decided, should be treated as necessities not luxuries, to be taken in moderation however they are needed, and not in excess.

I phoned Maurice Bridgeland and told him, as I had done before, that I had not achieved anything over the last ten years. Maurice responded by saying he thought I had achieved more than some people had achieved over the last ten years', this was similar to what he had said before when I had complained about not having done anything. He had responded then by saying, considering my problems I had, I had achieved a lot. I told him I now needed to work a lot harder and that Bill Thompson had told me I had a huge amount to catch up on. This was something Maurice had agreed with.

'You do have a huge amount to catch up on, Bill.' He meant I had a huge amount to catch up on in the way I thought and behaved, not just the things I had not done. The things I had done, such as laughing to myself, dancing around in Maurice's office, having tantrums and daydreaming, these were all things that I had wasted time on. These were not just things that were meaningless and useless, but were actually harmful to myself and had led to having bad concentration in everyday life; they also made me look bad. I felt I was beginning from absolutely nothing in terms of mental, financial and emotional well-being, work experience and career plans. I told Maurice this.

'You're beginning from the background you have of a stable home.'

I had set myself goals that I had not set before, except when practising my kung fu with the instructor. 'You have to practise at home,' he had told me, and I had.

I was now more aware of the important things in life and what was necessary for everyday life, such as where to get money if you did not work, who was to pay for lodgings, clothes, etc. I wanted to make lists of all the things I needed to find out and attend to. I went down to the nearest DHSS office in Commercial Road to find out about benefits and what I was entitled to if unemployed.

Being unemployed now began to depress me as it had not done before as I now realised that benefits and being kept by the state was not necessarily the natural order of things. I realised the struggle of everyday life that, from a certain age, demanded everything a person had. I realised that practical took precedence over the personal and emotional, that the personal and emotional development come after practical concerns. Importantly, I felt I was changing deep down; being broken down and rebuilt mentally and emotionally; I was parting with daydreaming and fantasy.

Bill Thompson had told me that daydreaming and fantasy were no use to me unless I was writing a book, and could express my imagination through that.

I started writing a novel about one of the daydreams I had had; it concerned Lancelot in the time of King Arthur – in this case he was an 8th century British warrior rather than an English knight, and he was made immortal by Merlin, to emerge in the 20th century. It may have been sub-conscious and inadvertent that it was really a rip-off of the film *Highlander*, which also dealt with immortality. I would spend hours at my desk writing, having no sense of time. I did not keep up with how many words I wrote and how many pages I filled, I now had a huge amount of motivation that I released on to paper.

Many of the early parts of the novel were very vivid and poetically visual, especially in the descriptions of swirling battle scenes and acts of magic carried out by Merlin and the story's villain, Prince Mallonea of Eire. The parts of the writing I had most trouble with were the parts involving communication between the characters. The dialogue was very stilted and awkward, it was also very vague. The characters spoke in an over-introspective way, their words and sentences were not related to anything that actually happened. One of the scenes involving sustained dialogue between two characters, Guinevere and another woman, were concerned with inner feelings and thoughts rather than anything more direct; this was an expression of my own introspective nature that considered thoughts rather than actions and things.

I had told Bill Thompson about my being introspective, rather than doing things for the last ten years.

'That's exactly what we shouldn't be doing in that time.'

I felt I was breaking out of myself, tearing through the metal walls around me; I was now even more aware of being introspective, along with many other things.

The other reason the dialogue between the characters was poor, was because it was written by someone who lacked background understanding of what people said, and how they communicated with each other. I did not understand how people's thoughts and statements were affected by the situation around them and how they would practically respond to it. I would write endlessly the pages of the novel; when I got up to the part where Lancelot died in battle and was brought back to life by Merlin as immortal, then I got stuck. I could not think of any more to write and so I gave up after writing 3,000 words.

I was going to bed early and getting up early. I would sit in the dining room with the fire on, brooding over what had happened and what to do about it.

Whilst writing my novel, I had also been attending a confidence-building course. I had told the group and the organiser that I was attending it in order to be confident as a next step in what I wanted to do. The fact that I had gone on a self-confidence course was a sign that I was prepared to face the fact that I was not confident.

The other people there were mainly women, who were mainly late middle-aged and elderly. There were two other blokes there besides me, one bloke a year younger than me who was going just to achieve confidence in some parts of his life, and another bloke who, from the outset, was rather odd. I met him a few other times after the confidence course ended. He wore a woolly hat and his name was Peter; he was poorly dressed and had a twitch.

Peter claimed when I spoke to him, that he had a mental state that affected his thinking and his outlook. He said he hated a lot of everyday institutions like the services and psychiatrists; a lot of the ones that made up society. Peter said that unless something happened in the future he would be as disassociated from society and as confused as he had always been. I later thought that we both had different problems; his was the past and the future, mine was just the past.

One night when I was meeting the self-confidence group, a few days after I had received the awakening from Bill Thompson, I had been sitting in a circle that made up the group when I asked to be excused – I was very uptight in how I seemed to the others, almost traumatised. Peter must have realised this because he followed me to the toilet where I threw up. He had followed me out of concern, and was shocked when I threw up all over a urinal.

'I have problems too, Bill,' he stated. 'I actually know I'm going to do something stupid,' he had mentioned one time during the week when he had lost five pounds.

'What, so your problems are worse than mine?' I had asked clumsily.

'Well,' Peter stopped at this. 'I wouldn't say mine are worse.' Peter did have problems for which he had refused psychiatric help; psychiatrists were part of the society he rejected, but at least he had more social understanding than me.

On the night I was in my distraught mood during the course, I told the organiser I was upset about all the time I had wasted;

she thought that no time is wasted, I did not know whether to agree with her. A friend of our family told me it was best if we were faced with two opposite viewpoints so we could then find a middle way. I told her about future career plans I could have; she told me that she once wanted to be a vet but the college she was at did not have a course for it. At this time I decided to put out of my head any thoughts that I had some sort of 'problem' that I did not know about; I no longer wanted to use it as an excuse.

'You've got two alternatives, Bill,' Bill Thompson had told me. 'You can either delude yourself you've got some sort of problem and use it as an excuse not to do anything, or you can start doing things. If you start doing things you'll have to face the fact you haven't done anything over the past ten years, and thus you've lost all those opportunities.' I was now faced with the latter and was having to deal with it.

I had told the organiser of the self-confidence group when we were in the pub, (we were celebrating the end of the course), that I had felt like hitting her; it was part of the pent-up frustration I had felt all my life that was now being released, as well as added to. She asked me what she had done to upset me. I knew she had done nothing; it was not her fault the way I felt. I had told Bill Thompson the same thing in the row we had towards the end of the public speaking course.

'Want a fight do you?' Bill Thompson had responded 'Cause if you do, Kiddo, I will get you first,' he had warned me. Again, it was pent-up frustration that had caused me to threaten him.

All this was happening the same week the Denmead Potteries course ended and I was no longer eligible for the PETA training course, following an incident when I had nearly come close to doing what I threatened to do to Bill and the confidence course organiser. One of the supervisors had been discussing the course with me when something had come over me and snapped, and I had thrust my fist to within a few inches of his face. He had thrown me out of the office and I had returned around forty-five minutes later to meet fairly sympathetic but regretful supervisors who told me I was no longer eligible for the scheme.

Chapter 19

Joining the Navy

A few days after the breakdown, if that is what it had been, I decided to try to join the Navy; I was desperate and could not think of many other things to do for a career.

When I had told my parents this, my father had said to go ahead if it meant a job, but then said I was not 'alert' enough. I was to later find out about what would be required of me in any of the services plus what I could enjoy from the services themselves; it was something I would become more aware of. The effects of my experience had become noticed by my family; the night after the night of the incident, I had come home shocked and had gone to a local youth hostel to sleep. I had not told my mother where I was going, and consequently she had been seriously worried when I did not come home; she was very angry when I finally came home the following morning.

I still watched some television; it was alright I had told myself at the time, providing I did not watch too much. I still allowed myself other luxuries like buttered toast with Marmite. It seemed, the more my constant habits were challenged by disruption and traumas, the more I would try and make them remain the same; it was partly the desire for pleasure, and to a greater extent the autistic desire for 'sameness' in everyday happenings.

I entered the Navy Recruiting Office, off Commercial Road

in the very state that made me more motivated, however, this was also the very state that was making me seem confused and uncoordinated; I was confused and uncoordinated. The Navy officers were behind a long desk, interviewing several prospective recruits. The officer speaking to me was a charming Petty officer who asked me my name, which I gave, then asked me my age.

'Twenty-three,' I told him.

'Oh,' he reacted. Then, 'Ancient,' he joked. I was seated opposite him across a desk; he seemed to react positively when I told him I had two GCSEs. He gave me a date of when a recruiting test was being held at HMS Nelson, near the Hard and also told me I needed to bring a prescription for the glasses I wore.

On the way out I saw another bloke being interviewed; he did not seem as bright as me, or as some blokes. He was sitting opposite an officer saying haltingly that he wanted to be a deckhand or 'swabby'. I realised that, less-bright seeming as he was, he at least knew more than I did about 'swabbies' in the Navy. It was one of the general details I was less aware of.

As instructed, I had gone to HMS Nelson on a cold, windy morning a few days later. We all gathered at the gatehouse at the entrance to the Naval base; there were twenty, twenty-five of us. The men there were all younger than me, like the man I had seen in the office. There was a checkpoint nearby with a Marine guarding it. After around an hour's wait, we were woken up by the crack of a Petty Officer's voice.

'Right!'

There was a younger naval officer besides the Petty Officer who said, 'If you'll come this way.'

'Right,' the Petty Officer repeated. We filed behind the two officers, following them from the guardhouse to one of the big main buildings and found ourselves in what seemed to be a large hall or gymnasium. There were a lot of tables and chairs assembled in front of each other in rows, and placed on each table there was a pencil and piece of paper.

One of the Naval officers stood at the front of our row of seats and told us we had around an hour and a half to complete the question paper in front of us. There were a number of questions on the page that could be answered by ticking off a particular letter; this was explained to us by the officer who ended by asking, 'Is there anyone who does not understand this?' This was the literally minded approach that was part of the military mentality. I understood the instructions perfectly. The military mentality went into detail on a practical level; it wanted to understand things one at a time, and in order. I could understand simple things but I could not understand some simple things at speed. The approach of the Naval officers was exact and patient.

We were told to start writing; the whole atmosphere of the test was like one of a school exam and for the next ninety minutes there was silence.

Most of the paper was easy for me, despite being in my fairly confused mental and emotional state, which might have made it difficult for me to concentrate. The easiest part of the paper I found was on grammar and English; I had always found English and grammar so easy that I found it rather odd as to why other people didn't.

When the ninety minutes were up, the officer announced it, and then announced that someone would collect our papers. Our papers were collected, then we were told an officer would go through our papers, study them and we would be called to an officer who would speak to us about our results. We waited for about an hour; the officers were on one side of the hall at tables reading our papers and we were milling around the other side chatting to each other. Eventually an officer, the same amiable-seeming Petty Officer I had met in the recruiting office, called me to his table and asked me to take the seat that was on the other side. He told me simply from the beginning that I had failed the test; I remember leaving some questions unanswered because I had not time to finish them. Apparently, the test had involved speed as well as concentration; I had been required to think and concentrate at speed. Unfortunately for me, if I did something too quickly I made mistakes, if I did something too slowly I lost time. The Navy Petty Officer told me there were no positions available for people with my level of achievement. I was told I could come back next year to re-sit the test if I still wanted to join. I was allowed a free lunch at the base canteen before being obliged to leave.

I had considered the effect of what I was doing and the impact it would cause, and had imagined myself in a few months' time writing to Maurice from a navy vessel sailing the sea. It had seemed rather outrageous, the idea of me telling my parents I was in the Navy. It was the first time in my life that I had taken direct responsibility for myself by taking direct action. I had wanted to join the Navy because it sounded more glamorous than the Army and would be an alternative to being unemployed; in the past I had been excited by the idea of the services and the military, but had never considered myself becoming part of it.

I felt the real feeling of being unemployed, the feeling of misery and despair and could see the social situation of unemployment the way other people did. I saw the need for myself to work, more importantly the desire of myself to work, my wanting to use my everyday time in society better, as part of the time I had on the earth. It was for this brief period that

I had a feeling of how a person thought, I felt socially and emotionally about being jobless in society. This was part of an awareness of society and its conditions.

At this time, I had seriously considered leaving home; I did not know exactly why, it was just a feeling of greater motivation and a greater impulse for me to take action. I had looked through a number of advertisements for lodgings, I wanted somewhere cheap that would take in recipients of DHSS benefits.

There were a number of places I enquired at that all looked very cheap. The main place was just a basic set of two rooms that had just basic furnishings and very little real paint. I told Bill Thompson when he asked me what I was up to that I was thinking of moving out of home. He had been amused and had told me my parents were the best place I could be at the moment.

'Why? What for?' he had asked. 'Why move out when you can stay with your parents? Since it takes about twenty pounds to heat a student room you're better off where you are.'

I understood what he meant about how much it would cost to heat a room. I had been making lists myself about how much gas would cost, electricity would cost which, added on top of food and lodging, I was now more aware of the details that made up the reality of everyday living. I may have thought at the time that these were all details that no amount of petty enjoyments such as TV, sweets or the cinema could remove or deal with.

Chapter 20

Another course; More schemes

*I*n the aftermath of the Denmead Potteries scheme ending I was assigned to a career evaluation course, or something to that effect at a school in Havant. We had sat in a conference room at several tables arranged in a circle and there had been a board with sheets of paper on it. On the sheets of paper things had been written. I was with a number of other people. I was still in my hyped up mood, still tensed with my feelings of extreme motivation and anxiety. I had cut myself off socially at this time as I was more concerned with doing things and making plans than with talking to people. I would sit at my table while all the others chatted and made jokes. I was now considering not just whether I spoke to people but what I said to people and how.

I had been told by a bloke on the scheme, a middle-aged bloke, to 'cheer up'. I was looking gloomy because of my anguish. 'It may never happen,' the man said. 'Oh, it already has,' he joked. I was aware of the effect of smiling and not smiling had on people. I felt extremely motivated but did not know whether I seemed all that motivated to other people. I had felt a great urge to get involved with people and to behave the right way in front of others and had mentioned the issue of how I related to people to Bill Thompson. Bill Thompson told me not to be concerned so much with people, not at the expense of things such as a career and future plans for activities in life. He thought too much time spent thinking about relationships with others was time wasted. While sitting at my table in the room I had placed a chair on the floor upended – everyone else had been talking and joking. I had placed the chair down to do something socially, not to consciously seek a response from others but just out of social compulsion. My handling of the chair aroused little comment from the rest of the group.

I had been talking to another group of people who were on the course when one of them offered me a cigarette.

'No, I don't smoke,' I said, 'but I'll have yours.' This had been meant as a flippant comment but had created a slightly puzzled response from the bloke I had said it to. It was my attempt to imitate the way I had heard them speak to each other.

I met a careers officer to discuss my future career plans and future employment at the end of the careers course. We sat in an office and she had told me that what concerned her most was the fact that I did not talk enough. I myself did not think it was all that important and said it was just as important to understand the job and concentrate on it. The woman had said, she was very concerned, that being relatively young I could be expected to have a more dynamic aspect to my character. By this she meant a more relaxed, outgoing personality, which involved mingling with people more and talking to them. She associated it with young people and it was exactly the sort of quality I had noticed in young people. The quality of interacting energetically, especially with each other comes about, I have theorised, from young people becoming more aware of each other and the world about them. A seventeen-year-old for example who began playing with other children around the age of ten would have seven years of emotional and mental development to experience. By the time they had reached seventeen, they would have had a lot of mental and emotional experiences behind them, because of that social interaction.

The years ten to seventeen might be considered crucial as they were the years that paralleled physical maturity, and paid host to mental and emotional maturity generally. People who experienced this would probably be more confident than me, precisely because they had experienced these mental, emotional and social changes. They experienced a sense of being, the same sort of sense of knowing that I had experienced, only I had experienced it at around twenty-one years of age, whereas they had experienced it a lot younger.

The careers officer suggested spending more time with people my own age or younger, around sixteen to twenty, and she even suggested the possibility of a youth club if I was not too old. I kept saying I considered doing a job itself more important; the woman had thought a more dynamic attitude important to fit in with fellow employees, and to make an impression on the boss.

The interview ended with me leaving without any idea of how I could get employment or what sort of employment I wanted. My father walked into the building to talk to the woman; she probably repeated what she had said to me to my father. My father had, I seem to think, told her about what he considered to be my sad past; being bullied by girls at school and leaving school seven years earlier. He was sad at what he thought was my last chance at employment.

I had disregarded the social aspect of work that the woman had focused on because I was more concerned with the practical aspects of concentrating on a job and being able to think about the job without making mistakes.

The job scheme had been unable to find anything for me so they put me in the direction of a job club, which was located at a community centre on the way to Southampton. The job club had begun with a course that lasted a few days and was similar to what I had experienced on other schemes. We were given a few lessons on interview techniques; one of us would play the part of an interviewer, the other the interviewee. Apart from myself on the short course, there was a middle-aged woman and a lad younger than me by four years. The course was held in a room just above the community centre. The woman who took us on the course was a dark-haired, attractive Scotswoman, she would occasionally show flashes of irritation with me because I was frequently late and seemed to lack initiative; she would have to place a piece of paper in front of me when I needed to write a letter to an employer. I was very motivated inside myself and the motivation was meant to be channelled into certain areas; I was more concerned with the large scale of things, such as making big decisions that would affect my life.

At the time I would have said I did not want a job I wanted a career – the incident and acquaintance with Bill Thompson had encouraged me to think in ambitious terms. One reason I had come to think in ambitious terms may have been because of all the pent up energy that had developed in my first twenty-three years of life – all the energy had developed into broad ambition rather than anything channelled or focused upon everyday things such as greater concentration and hobbies.

I once had to phone the woman up at the job club; I was already late. When I spoke to her she was immediately angry and said she would make me write a letter about why I was late – if I was late again. Eventually, because she could not find employment for me and because she wanted to get rid of me anyway, she suggested I apply to a temporary agency.

The first of the temporary agencies I was to apply to was called Brook Street. I went into the office and gave them my name and all my details. I was assigned to a Postal centre near the bottom of Portsmouth; it was simple work, sorting out parcels. I had never considered in my own mind parcels and the post office, but it seemed to be quite impressive in the first few days, more so because I had a lot of natural drive within me that was being released in a situation that demanded it.

I was required to show energy and initiative in a job situation. I placed parcels in particular places and pushed trolleys full of parcels to other parts of the centre. At the beginning of one shift, my workmates had told me they had requested me to be sent down because I was reliable. I knew I was reliable; I was making an effort to do certain things without being told to do them and to do things without considering whether I needed to do them – my motivation was making up for my lack of my concentration.

My thoughts were suspended by my being on a higher level of motivation. Rather than think of what had to be done I guided myself to do it through an almost instinctive higher level of feeling. My motivation, I realised, was still not up to the same level as other people's; it was not as continual and not as latent, I had to practise it to perfect it. I almost thought that other people had longer experience than I had of being motivated, through longer experience of outside stimulus. I felt I had cut myself off from outside stimulus through cutting myself off from the outside.

My motivation began to flag when I was required to unload a lorry. The driver I was unloading it with complained I did not unload enough parcels in one go, he said I was picking them up one by one and putting them on the conveyor belt leading from the lorry. The driver told me he would be late at his next destination because of me and complained badly. Even my colleagues who normally worked with me and applauded me as efficient became sarcastic and said, 'I thought this was voluntary work.'

The problem was, I had been so motivated over the past few months from February to May that the time had seemed to go more quickly. This had scared me as I felt time would continue to go more quickly, eventually taking up my entire life before I achieved all the big things that I wanted to achieve. When I told my father this he said, 'Oh, you mean you think you're getting older and not achieving anything?' He was partly alluding to what I had mentioned to him earlier from the age of twelve or thirteen. That if I started doing things, I would have to face the fact that I had not done things and thus, I had lost years of my life.

My entire outlook tended to be strange. The other jobs I did for the temporary agency were making money boxes at a factory, some cleaning jobs and working at a warehouse that stored curtain railings.

The cleaning job turned out very badly through no fault of mine, or possibly my disability. It was because I could not understand my supervisor's accent. He was an amiable Scot, a young man whom I drove almost to distraction; if I had understood him, I may have still had problems with speed and accuracy. My disability may have caused a partial problem by making me too slow to catch what a person said quickly enough; the Scots lad spoke quickly and sharply.

The Scots lad told me I would not be needed, so when I turned up the following morning he said to his boss, 'I told him he wouldn't be needed, honest I did.' I had not understood what he said; the cleaning job lasted only a few days.

The job at the warehouse went badly as well, though that was far more illuminating. I turned up there one morning; it was an enclosed building comprising the warehouse and office sections. There was an amiable middle-aged woman who met me. She directed me to a young man about a year younger than me, called Sean. Sean gave me jobs to do like putting away boxes full of screws and small cardboard boxes that I had to squeeze into metal shelves. I had to get cardboard boxes containing rails down from the top of the warehouse, they were on top of rafters and I had to get them down with a stick. All the while I did this Sean and the others were grinning at me, and looking at me in a strange way. I was curious about why they were behaving the way they did. There were two other blokes besides Sean, one was a bloke younger than me, about eighteen or nineteen, another was older, about thirty five or six.

When we broke for tea all three of them were laughing about something as we left our work to sit in another part of the warehouse.

As we sat resting, Sean looked at me, grinning and asked, 'Have you done all your...,' he paused for effect, 'little jobs?' He was almost on the point of hysterical laughter along with the other two.

Later I was to realise what they were laughing at; they were laughing at me. It was as I had wanted to tell the woman at the employment rehabilitation centre, a person had to understand what needed to be done in a job in order to do it. They were laughing at me because I had not asked any of the things that were relevant to the job such as, 'Where do all the different rails go?', 'In what different part of the warehouse do they go?' I had not thought to myself, 'I'm working in a warehouse, if I'm working in a warehouse, what happens in a warehouse?'

My process of thought should have gone like this: 'What are warehouses for?' I ask myself. 'They are for keeping things in, storing them to be distributed throughout the country.' If this is true, then they receive items of whatever they are storing – cans of paint, garden implements, shoes, machinery parts, etc., and they also send them out. In summary: if a person works in a warehouse they load whatever stuff the warehouse stores on to trucks, these trucks drive off to distribute the stuff on to shelves – if they are receiving it.

I could have said to Sean when we sat down to tea, 'Right, now if there's stuff coming in there's stuff going out, right?' It would have been interesting to see the effect the words would have had on Sean and the others. It should have elicited some response from them that would at least have been partly positive.

Warehouses were things I had not thought about; they were one of the many everyday facets of society I had not been aware of. If I had been aware of warehouses, I had not seen the significance of them and their practical value to society.

The lads asked me how long I had been doing casual work, I told them a few weeks. They asked me what I had done before, I said the six months security job and before that the school caretaking job. Sean asked me how old I was, I told him I was twenty-three. Sean, a wedge-haircutted lad, who looked like Tommy Steel was shocked, along with the two others.

'You're twenty-three and you've never had a full-time job?' gasped Sean.

'You'd better pull your socks up,' said one of the other two, meaning I needed to get a full-time job to make up for lost time.

The next day I turned up for work I received fairly hostile

looks from the people working in the office section. I went into the warehouse section where Sean and the others were busy; there had been a large assortment of stuff that had come in. Sean and the two others were busy stapling down cardboard boxes. I was rushed in, a stapling device was stuck in my hand, and Sean threw me some cardboard pieces to put together for the curtain rails that they would contain.

I fitted the long pieces of cardboard, bending them over so they were a cylinder of four sides. I then had to fit another piece of cardboard into one end before it could be stapled. One moment of lapsed concentration, one second in which I failed to notice what Sean was doing meant one piece of cardboard was placed in the tube facing the wrong way up – the sides of the piece of cardboard, which had to be facing outwards and upwards were pointing downwards and inwards.

Sean was stapling them all when he found mine, which I now realised I had done wrongly. I heard him snarl, 'Stupid git,' meaning me. I had turned away to do something when I heard it.

I had heard the other two say some things about me before. One of them had been searching for the knives they carried to cut cardboard and said to his mate, 'I wonder if Dinlow's got it,' meaning me.

Another time, Sean had put a load of cardboard boxes containing curtain rails into my arms and said, 'Right, you know where these things go?'

'Yes,' I'd replied because I thought I knew where they went. I did not want to seem stupid to them, even though I seemed stupid to them anyway. The boxes Sean had given me were long and clumsy; I wandered round the warehouse as though I was expected to know without asking. After a few seconds I asked an elderly gentleman where they were supposed to go.

He pointed me to a part of the warehouse where there were cupboard-like installations, so I put them there.

'Did you know where they went?' Sean asked when he came up to me, he had heard me ask.

'No,' I replied, realising that I had not known.

'Then why did you say you did know when you didn't?'

If I had known what was required of me in the job, I would have asked Sean when he asked me if I knew. It was ironic – the fact that I had tried to cover up how stupid I was had made me act in a way that was even more stupid.

There was another bloke at the warehouse, he was Asian and I knew him from an assertiveness course that I was doing. At the end of one shift there was a choice between him and me to do some more shifts. Sean had automatically, naturally picked him but then decided to flip a coin for it. I won and turned up for the other shifts.

There were around three shifts that I did, the last shift was the last I did at all for Harrison Drapes. Sean had told me in the middle of work that I was no longer needed.

I turned up later at the job centre for advice on future employment and a future career; the place was the same place I had gone to earlier at the bottom of Cosham High Street just past the railway crossing.

The young man behind the desk had advised me to try a training scheme like I had done with the YTS. The training scheme I was told I could apply for was part of NACRO, The National Association for the Care and Rehabilitation of Offenders. The one-year scheme was to be held at a place near Havant. The headquarters of the scheme were next to a school that was quite large. The lad at the office in Cosham had told me it was better to try to get a full-time permanent job.

'Your temporary work is like a circle, Bill. The more

temporary work you do, the less time is spent looking for a full time job.'

We went through a usual introductory stage of two or three weeks where we sat round a table in a conference room drinking coffee and hearing lectures from people in charge of the scheme. We were lectured on things such as confidence, talent and choices.

There was a choice for me between insulation and gardening. At first I chose insulation, this involved insulating houses round their doors and widows. We would go round to people's houses doing this. The fellow leading our team was an Irishman from Belfast, who was constantly frustrated by me using too much plastic for the frames of the doors. We had long strips that we would place down the sides of the door and which we would then nail in place with a nail punch. The Irish leader of the team had to keep reminding me to cut the plastic to the right length; I would either cut it too long or too short.

'I've shown you and shown you,' the Irishman would say in despair. Eventually I was taken off cutting the plastic and not allowed to do it. I could not automatically judge where to cut the plastic. I would try to cut it short enough to fit against the bottom of the door but would leave a few inches from the bottom that would later allow a draught into the house.

The insulation of the houses continued for a few months. I did not seem to show much enthusiasm or motivation for it because, in our five person group, I could not decide whether to do insulation or gardening.

Eventually after a few months I was called into the scheme's main headquarters. There was a man who discussed with me what I had been doing and what decisions I had made. The scheme's organiser, a very pleasant man, pointed out to me from the very beginning that I did not seem confident, it was something I wanted to work on. I did not say it at the time but it was something I had always known. I was more concerned with other things, such as whether to 'let reality in'; whether to allow myself to interact with my everyday experiences and allow myself to be stimulated by them.

I discussed insulation with other men directing the scheme. One man mentioned that I did not want to do insulation, that is what he had presumed about me. Later, when asked, I said I wanted to do gardening.

I started off at an allotment near the school. I would be left there for hours sometimes with another bloke, or number of other blokes. We would sit there sometimes doing around half an hour's work in the whole day. We would occasionally be visited by a supervisor, in this case a middle-aged bald man with glasses on. It was summer and it got very hot; I would feel tired during the day because I stayed up late watching TV, often until eleven or twelve o'clock in the evening. My mother would end up shouting at me about whether I cared about the training scheme and if got there on time.

Staying up late and getting up late was part of what was holding me back, not allowing myself to be disciplined.

I would catch the bus to the centre every morning and arrive there on time but I had little to do.

There were other men who came on to gardening with me. One was a fat, curly-haired man who later proved to be a complete pain. He seemed reasonably friendly at first, but later, when we would be sitting around at the allotment he would wind me up. He would say things that were unusual and exaggerated about Russian submarines aboard planes. Sometimes he would be directly abusive.

'Go dig a deep hole, Bill, and jump into it.'

Later on, around five years later, I would have been able to make a retort. 'If you jumped in a big hole, you'd fill it.'

It would take me a long time to be able to deal with being wound up at work and elsewhere. I could cope with direct verbal abuse such as being sworn at, because I had experienced so much of it. In the past being, 'wound up' was different, because it was far more subtle, and in its way, more unsettling.

We would go on jobs out to places in the country – mainly labouring work such as digging ditches and repainting fences. One time, I spent time with a couple of men who were putting up a fence. I had been working with them hammering in nails with a two handed device – a large metal instrument that came over the nail, hammering it into the earth. One man stood on one side while another stood on the other, each holding a handle, they had to work in conjunction, both bringing it down together. I worked with the team leader for a few minutes but I could not bring the device down in unison with him. It felt to me that I was bringing it down at the same time but according to him, I wasn't. I could not immediately judge when to bring it down and when I went to bring it up, I could not think quickly enough.

The headquarters were beside the bridge and consisted of a large hut, which resembled a workshop for carpentry. There was a room at the side of the hut that had windows; the room was a classroom with tables and chairs. I had been part of a class in there that had taught additional English skills.

One day, when I passed, I saw a man sitting down in there who had a peculiar look in his eyes, it was an unfocused stare that had made him look menacing. At first, I thought he was some sort of criminal hard case – NACRO was for offenders and had been set up to rehabilitate them – but later, the man turned up at one of our sites and was helped out of the van by a couple of other men. The middle-aged supervisor came up to me and told me that the man coming out of the van was mentally handicapped – this was to prepare me for working with him. The supervisor had obviously said similar things to the other men.

The mentally handicapped man was very quiet and remote. I did not know what his precise mental handicap was, but by definition he seemed autistic in the sense that he did not talk to anyone very much, and his social contact was restricted. The man who often irritated me was very good to the mentally handicapped man when he first met him, he treated him with some understanding, in a courteous sensitive way.

'How are you Mike? Are you alright?' he asked when he first met Mike. Mike looked gloomy most of the time, though he would smile occasionally and his eyes would shine.

There were a number of lessons in the windowed room, given by a middle-aged English teacher. Mike was not in these lessons, he was taught separately. The English teacher later told me he found it hard to teach Mike, if not impossible. He told me it was very difficult for him to understand what Mike was understanding and taking in.

On one site, the same site I had been working with the fence-making device, the same man spoke rather harshly about Mike. I myself did not find what he said offensive, insensitive yes, but not offensive. Mike was not able to work out how to take down the fence we had put up. He would try to tear up the thing by the posts. I knew not to try and tear up the fence by its posts, but to remove the wire first from the poles. I knew in my confused way that whatever problem I had, it was not as serious as Mike's.

The teasing from the fat man eventually became too much, and after one particular incident, I was suspended from the scheme for a week.

This kind of 'winding up' would be easier for me to deal with later on; I could take it from a more confident and more socially aware viewpoint.

When I got back from the suspension, the fat man was friendlier.

Later the scheme ended.

Chapter 21

Eureka!!

'*I*'m not going to be on that scheme forever,' I had told my parents.

'That's very mature of you,' my father added darkly. The problem was, I was not independent and this, together with the lack of a job, was causing problems.

My brother had left home, and towards the end of that year my father had a stroke. The next year involved just roaming around Portsmouth on my own. I had things building up, and we eventually decided that I had to leave home. A social worker was contacted and he gave us the name of a couple who could put me up.

The Brimecombes were a late middle-aged couple who owned a house in the Eastney area of Portsmouth; the food was good and conditions adequate. Ma Brimecombe was forthright and very maternal; she would call me lazy and demand I do voluntary work at a garden centre. I explained to my social worker I wanted somewhere different to live, as I found my carer too bossy. He found me a new place with a couple of married carers; it was a residential home in Southsea.

There were several other people who arrived there over the years, all with learning disabilities. A fat, curly-haired man, a young man, supposedly with autism and a small woman with Down's Syndrome. The woman in charge was far less bossy than Mrs Brimecombe, but younger and more volatile. I was, and still am a sensitive person, and her tendency to speak excitedly and angrily made me nervous.

Over the next five years carers would come and ask me how I liked being at the place; I was too nervous to say I did not like being snapped at by either of the people in charge. The food was still good, and a new man arrived called Kevin Sheath who was good at communicating with others. He had, I later realised, high emotional intelligence, despite being intellectually below par. He was also a lot less sensitive than I was in that he was far less nervous about being shouted at.

At twenty-seven years-old I had another kind of short-lived breakdown. I could not decide certain things such as whether to join one of the services. I spent two years as an adult student at a learning centre, the Grove. The course involved writing and general artistic expression – it was the best two years of my life. Everyone was so sensitive and supportive. I overheard a teacher mention how mature and assertive she thought I had become. The aggressive feelings I had, from twenty-seven onwards, had been channelled into something that was thinking more about what was around me, what was going on and rationalising it. This gave me the ability to rationally and logically examine individual situations.

There was an incident when one man called me stupid because I could not work out how to use a tea machine, showing my lack of practical intelligence. In another incident I snogged a girl when the teacher was out of the room. She might have had problems herself; I got into trouble because of it. Snogging the girl was down to my curiosity about sex.

I was good at acting and painting, being described as a competent actor by my drama teacher, and was witty and funny, according to another teacher.

On leaving the Grove I embarked on History, Drama and Psychology courses at Portsmouth College and gained a GCSE in Psychology and later an 'AS' level. I also achieved an AS in History. The social side of college was stable apart from one incident I had with a girl who told me off for picking my nose in class. Later on, I could have explained it was lack of social insight. During this time, I held down a paper round I had had since I was thirty years old that paid me some extra money.

The second year of the drama course came up; it was January and bitingly cold to be going out every morning in gloves and a woolly hat. I had been toying with the idea of becoming an actor; I knew I had talent but at 32 years old I thought I maybe too old.

A huge amount had been building up and the cold weather made me groggy. A big decision, the first ever big decision in my life was hammering away at me. I decided to try to sort out my problems by writing them down; I had been having suicidal thoughts at the back of my mind, involving a railway station I frequently passed.

I began to write, it eventually turned to my past experiences. As I wrote the words, their symmetry began to take on a pattern and a new realisation began to form. *You're autistic*, a voice screamed; liberating me from what? I began to write more and more, faster and faster about my life and experiences, aching, a kind of euphoria.

'Yooouuuuu're autistic!!!!'

It was a huge accidental self diagnosis that may have saved my life. I worked day and night on the writing, only sleeping when I needed to. In a few days I had produced a substantial amount of work, since then I have become more tenacious in what I do.

When I was thirty, I had been considered more assertive,

and I continue with that assertion still. I have become involved with various groups including an amateur dramatics society; I have twice travelled to China to take part in two charity events; I have also tried finding a girlfriend.

After '32 years imprisonment', I had realised my condition.

Postscript

While most of what you have read may seem depressing, I gain solace from the time when I was sitting in the bathroom brooding over the evil done to me by others. I experienced my whole self coming together, and my eyes opening, rather than my bowels. I became briefly aware of the world and its existence, also aware of my own existence in relation to the world around me. This is the key to my future.